SCIENTIFIC AMERICAN™

Critical Anthologies on Environment and Climate™

CRITICAL PERSPECTIVES ON
PLANET EARTH

Edited by Jennifer Viegas

The Rosen Publishing Group, Inc., New York

Published in 2007 by The Rosen Publishing Group, Inc.
29 East 21st Street, New York, NY 10010

The articles in this book first appeared in the pages of *Scientific American*, as
follows: "Spring Forward" by Daniel Grossman, January 2004; "On Thin Ice?"
by Robert A. Bindschadler and Charles R. Bentley, December 2002; "Making
Every Drop Count" by Peter H. Gleick, February 2001; "Madagascar's
Lemurs" by Ian Tattersall, January 1993; "The Puzzle of Declining Amphibian
Populations" by Andrew R. Blaustein and David B. Wake, April 1995; "On
the Termination of Species" by W. Wayt Gibbs, November 2001; "Human
Population Grows Up" by Joel E. Cohen, September 2005; "Population,
Poverty and the Local Environment" by Partha S. Dasgupta, February 1995;
"Environmental Change and Violent Conflict" by Thomas F. Homer-Dixon,
Jeffrey H. Boutwell, and George W. Rathjens, February 1993; "The Industrial
Ecology of the 21st Century" by Robert A. Frosch, September 1995;
"Rethinking Green Consumerism" by Jared Hardner and Richard Rice, May
2002; "More Profit with Less Carbon" by Amory B. Lovins, September 2005;
"Urban Planning in Curitiba" by Jonas Rabinovitch and Josef Leitman, March
1996; and in the pages of *Scientific American Presents: The Oceans*, as follows:
"The World's Imperiled Fish" by Carl Safina, 1998.

First Edition

Library of Congress Cataloging-in-Publication Data

Critical perspectives on planet earth/edited by Jennifer Viegas.—1st ed.
    p. cm.—(Scientific American critical anthologies on environment and climate)
Includes bibliographical references and index.
ISBN 1-4042-0687-6 (library binding)
1. Climatic changes—Environmental aspects—Juvenile literature. I. Viegas,
Jennifer. II. Series.

QH543.V54 2007
333.72—dc22

                                                          2005031477

Manufactured in the United States of America

On the cover: A view of the varied terrain near the village of Cabra Cancha,
Bolivia.

CONTENTS

Introduction

Change is an inevitable part of life. As we age, our bodies change. In any given instant, the cells in our bodies undergo various processes, including cycles that affect our health, our appearance, and our moods. Birds, plants, insects, and animals have their own life cycles that intertwine with our lives. Most scientists believe all living things on Earth share a common ancestor, which over millions of years evolved into the diverse life-forms that now exist on our planet. Because of these cycles of change, we are all part of a giant ecosystem that spans the globe and possibly extends into the universe.

Although natural disasters can exert sudden and dramatic changes, nature usually works on a slow, steady timetable. A stream in a remote area, for example, will by itself change the landscape over time, but the differences likely will be subtle, with little impact on the animals and plants that live near the stream. Any changes, such as the wearing away of the stream's banks, will probably be gradual enough to allow life in the area to adapt.

Humans generally operate on a faster schedule. A group of people could dam up the stream or fill it with dirt to suit some need of theirs, such as a new shopping mall or housing development. Such changes happen frequently in urban areas, where humans have altered most inland bodies of water. In this case, we can adapt to the change, but other creatures may not be able to cope. Animals that once drank from the stream might not be able to find other water sources. Frogs and other amphibians that laid their eggs in the stream could die off, as might any fish that inhabited the waters. The loss of one small stream could hurt dozens of species.

Changes like this are taking place all over the planet. People are cutting down forests to supply lumber for housing. They are putting landfills in coastal regions for vacation spots and housing developments. Automobiles and power plants spew pollutants into the air, where they can collect in water droplets and fall back to Earth as acid rain. Open areas are being carved and paved over to create roads that will service more and more drivers. Rain forests are disappearing, in part, because locals are burning them down to establish farmlands.

For decades, we have known that human activities can lead to environmental problems, but data gathered in recent years is creating a clearer picture of what these problems may be. This anthology presents an overview of many pressing issues that face us now and will continue to plague us in the future unless solutions are found and implemented.

The first subject addressed in this collection is global climate change. Weather changes from day to day, but when these differences accumulate over a period, certain patterns begin to emerge. Most scientists agree that Earth has warmed up by at least one degree Fahrenheit (one-half degree Celsius) since the late nineteenth century. Melting glaciers, lower snowpacks in the Northern Hemisphere, and underground measurements all suggest that things are heating up.

Although our planet's climate has varied during the course of its history, many experts believe the current warming trend is unprecedented and is attributable to human activities. The warming occurs because pollution in the form of greenhouse gases stays in the atmosphere above us for decades and even centuries. To get an idea of what kind of pollution may encircle Earth, imagine being in a closed, windowless warehouse with several idling automobiles. Before long, the warehouse would fill with fumes. People would have to evacuate, or else they would run out of air to breathe.

Our atmosphere is not an entirely closed system like a shut warehouse, but pollution does not magically disappear either. Each time you ride in a car, plane, or bus that runs on fossil fuels, at least three groups of potentially deadly pollutants are released into the atmosphere. These include hydrocarbons that react with both sunlight and nitrogen oxides in the air to form ground level ozone, which is a reactive form of oxygen. When ozone forms naturally in the upper atmosphere, it helps to protect Earth from harmful ultraviolet rays emitted by the sun. When it forms because of human activities closer to ground level, ozone may harm human health by polluting the air that we breathe.

Nitrogen oxides also are released when fossil fuel, such as gasoline, burns in an engine. Aside from reacting with hydrocarbons, these compounds add to acid rain problems and can pollute water sources. Finally, use of fossil fuels creates a buildup of carbon monoxide, a colorless, odorless, yet deadly gas. Several medical studies show that carbon monoxide can reduce the flow of oxygen in the bloodstream and impair mental functions. In urban areas, up to 90 percent of detected carbon monoxide is due to motor vehicles.

Such pollution, combined with habitat loss, is devastating many of the world's animal and plant species. The second chapter in this anthology looks at Earth's threatened wildlife. Lemurs, for example, exist in the wild in only a single country, Madagascar. Since Madagascar is one of the world's poorest countries, locals both kill the animals for meat and cause deforestation through old slash-and-burn forms of agriculture, where forest areas are literally burnt to the ground before crops are sown. As a result, many lemur species have gone extinct. Several other species are now endangered.

Complicating the matter is our soaring population, the third subject of this book. In the next fifty years, humans will number approximately 9 billion. Imagine if your household doubled or even tripled in size. There would be less food and fewer resources for everyone. Space would be tight. Sacrifices would have to be made. Conflicts would arise due to heated tempers. That is what is happening on a global scale today.

The final subject addressed in this anthology concerns possible solutions to these profound and seemingly insurmountable problems. The restructuring of Curitiba in Brazil should give us all hope. Curitiba is a modern, populated city, but progressive leadership redesigned it with nature in mind. Instead of working against nature, architects and other city planners constructed houses and other necessary structures in ways that would minimally affect the environment. As the writer of the article states, "there is no time like the present" to enact positive change.

The existence of the human race is just a blip in Earth's history. Consider that dinosaurs lived on

Earth for about 165 million years. Most scientists believe our species, *Homo sapiens*, has been in existence for only about 200,000 years. During that relatively short time, we have managed to weaken and damage most of the complex and interrelated ecosystems on the planet. Nature may have its own slower timetable, but time is of the essence if we are to ensure both our future and the future of all of the other living things that share our planet. —*JV*

1 The Effects of Climate Change

Scientists who take a conservative view of climate change often suggest that the measured warming at Earth's surface may not directly affect certain plants and animals. As the following article indicates, however, these species may be indirectly hurt if their food supply diminishes. In this case, the food consists of winter moth caterpillars that chicks of a bird called the great tit feed upon.

The author alludes to the saying "The early bird gets the worm." Here it could be added that only the early birds get the worms, and those that do not, perish. This is because climate change likely causes the worm supply to peak two weeks earlier, providing only the earliest-hatched chicks with a reliable food source.

An interesting fact to keep in mind while reading this piece is that some of the data was collected by an individual who meticulously recorded the timing of bird arrivals at his home each spring. The Audubon Society and other organizations often sponsor annual bird counts. You and any other interested person can participate.

Contact your local Audubon chapter or bird watchers club for details. —JV

"Spring Forward"
by Daniel Grossman
Scientific American, **January 2004**

Growing up in England in the 1950s, Alastair Fitter spent a lot of time wandering with his father through the countryside near their home. The elder Fitter, Richard, now 90, is a noted naturalist (who has written almost three dozen books on flowers, birds and related topics). As a hobby, Richard jotted down the first flowering date of hundreds of plant species, the spring arrival time of scores of birds, the late-summer departure dates of butterflies, and other signs of the passing seasons. Richard, who insists that he is simply "an inveterate list maker," never thought the records would serve any scientific purpose: "When I was 10, I read I should be keeping notes."

Alastair grew up to be a naturalist like his father as well as a professor of ecology at York University. His father's notes, he realized as an adult, were one of the few cases in which a single observer had systematically recorded the timing details of so many species in one place for so long. So in 2001, when the elder Fitter moved from his home, the locus of 47 years of systematic observations in one place, Alastair decided to take a closer look at the scribblings. By then, climate researchers had confirmed that the earth is getting warmer with stunning speed. The near-surface temperature of the planet has risen about 0.6 degree Celsius (about 1.1 degrees Fahrenheit) in the past 100 years. The 1990s was the warmest decade on record. He thought his father's data might confirm with plant life what researchers had shown with thermometers.

What Alastair Fitter discovered astonished him. An analysis of the records that he had done in the early 1990s had not shown a consistent pattern. But comparing flowering dates for the entire decade of the 1990s with those of the previous four decades, he found that 385 plants were flowering an average of 4.5 days

Overview/*Ecosystems Under Stress*

- The recent surge in warming at the planet's surface has begun to alter the relationships among species in some ecosystems by weakening links in the food chain—between, for example, birds and the caterpillars they eat.
- Although the examples are not definitive, the signs are troubling, and many species could be at risk.
- Adding to the concern is research showing that the changing climate at the end of the last ice age tore apart existing ecosystems and created new ones, leaving no haven for species that no longer fit in.

earlier [*see illustration on opposite page*]. A smaller subset, 60 species in all, flowered on average two full weeks earlier, an astounding change for a single decade. It shows that, at least in the neighborhood of Oxford, England, "climate change is happening with extreme suddenness," Richard Fitter says.

The research, which the Fitters published jointly in *Science* in 2002, was only one of the more startling of a number of recent studies showing rapidly occurring changes in the life patterns of the world's plants and animals. Also in 2002 the Intergovernmental Panel on Climate Change (IPCC) published an overview of this topic based on a review of 2,500 published papers. A number of these articles reported on the relation between species and temperature for at least the past 20 years. Of the more than 500 birds, amphibians, plants and other organisms studied in these publications, 80 percent had changed the timing of reproduction or migration, length of growing season, population size or population distribution in ways that might be expected from warming temperatures. The overview's authors concluded that "there has been a discernible impact of regional climate change, particularly increases in temperature, on biological systems in the 20th century."

As with the Fitters' study of plant flowering, most of the studies reviewed by the IPCC did not investigate whether changes have been or will be harmful, but Alastair Fitter nonetheless believes adverse effects are inevitable: "When things flower may be relatively innocuous. Whether things go extinct is not, and that's going to be the next stage."

A small group of studies is taking up the challenge of looking into whether global warming is having an adverse effect on the relations among plants and animals within ecosystems. The research is proving that, in some cases, Fitter's gloomy prophecy is already becoming a reality: rising temperatures are degrading the links of food chains and the fitness of some creatures to continue to live in their habitats. In at least one

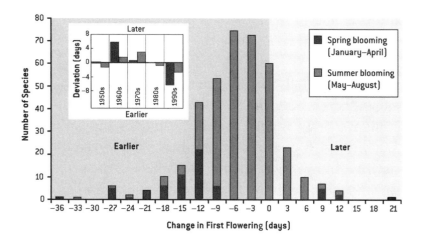

First flowering dates of 385 plant species from 1991 to 2000—the warmest decade on record—were an average of 4.5 days ahead of the 1954-to-1990 mean. For clarity, two species with extreme deviations, *Lamium album* [−55 days] and *Buddleja davidii* [+36 days] are omitted. A graph of the first flowering for each decade compared with the long-term mean (1954–2000) underscores the change that occurred in the 1990s (*inset*).

instance, a researcher predicts that global warming will extirpate one species from an entire region within 15 years. Although the data are insufficient so far to prove that many ecosystems are coming apart, the findings already point in a disturbing direction.

Earliest Birds and the Worm

In a small office at the Netherlands Institute of Ecology, not far from Arnhem, Marcel E. Visser is crawling under a table. Visser is the head of the institute's animal-population biology department. Right now he is stalking a small chickadeelike bird that entered the room through an open window. But before the scientist can grab the bird or shoo it out, the frightened animal takes flight and leaves of its own accord.

Coincidentally, the intruder was a great tit, the subject of a long-term study that Visser heads. The study was not designed to investigate global warming. When Visser's predecessors instituted the research in the 1950s, it was intended to contribute to the general understanding of bird populations. Under Visser's leadership, however, the research has become one of the only studies in the world examining the cascading effects of global warming on a food chain.

Great tits at De Hoge Veluwe National Park, a large wooded area near Visser's office, engage in their annual nesting rituals in April and May. At the same time, Visser engages in his own rites of spring, monitoring these birds and their offspring. The scientist and a crew of assistants record the activities and health of every breeding pair in about 400 wooden birdhouses in the park. One mid-May morning, carrying a short aluminum ladder on his shoulder, the ornithologist mounts a sturdy yellow bike and sets off over the park's unpaved paths.

After several minutes of pedaling, he parks his bike by a nest box mounted a few feet above eye level in a spindly oak. With help from the ladder, he scales the tree, installs a metal trap in the box and waits a short distance away. Within moments the trap catches one of the two adults that nest in the box. Visser carefully swings the top open and removes the bird. It has a gray back, a black-and-white head and a pale yellow breast with a black stripe and weighs only about as much as a AA battery. Gently he locks the bird's head between his pointer and middle finger and makes some measurements with a ruler. He weighs the tiny animal in a sandwich bag. Multiplied thousands of times a season, these statistics are critical raw material for Visser's research. He and his colleagues visit each box weekly except as hatching (and, later, fledging) approaches, when they make daily checks.

What Visser has found sounds harmless enough: the tits laid their eggs at almost the same time last year as they did in 1985. But over this same period, spring temperatures in the area have climbed, especially during the mid-spring (between April 16 and May 15), which has seen a warming of two degrees C. And although the chronology of the tits has not changed with this warming, that of winter moth caterpillars—

which (along with other less abundant species) tits feed their chicks—has [*see illustration on page 22*]. Caterpillar biomass—or the total meat available to the birds—peaks two weeks earlier today than it did in 1985. Back then, it occurred almost precisely when the tit hatchlings needed it most. Now, by the time most chicks have hatched, the caterpillar season is on the wane and food is becoming scarce. Only the earliest chicks get the worms.

It is not just the birds and the moths in this food web that are getting out of synchrony, or "decoupled," as Visser likes to say. The scientist also looks lower down the food chain to the relation between the moth and its food—young, tender oak leaves. To survive, the moth's caterpillar must hatch almost precisely at "bud burst," when the oaks' leaves open. If the insect hatches more than about five days before bud burst, it will starve. It will also starve if it hatches more than two weeks too late, because oak leaves become infused with inedible (to the caterpillar) tannin. Visser has discovered that at the De Hoge Veluwe park, oak bud burst now occurs about 10 days earlier than it did 20 years ago. Caterpillars hatch 15 days earlier, over-compensating by five days for the change in the oaks. The caterpillars were already hatching several days before bud burst in 1985, so now they must wait on average about eight days for food.

Visser's research shows that the winter moth population at De Hoge Veluwe is declining, but he has not collected moth numbers long enough to be sure this is not part of a natural cycle. The gap between the schedules of the caterpillars and the birds has had no demonstrable effect so far on tit numbers. The scientist says that could be because normal year-to-year fluctuations caused by various factors such as the availability of winter food are greater so far than the impact of warming. In a system where "timing is everything," however, Visser observes that the decoupling between links in the food chain cannot continue growing without consequence. "It's only a matter of time before we see the population come down," he says of the birds.

According to Visser, what is most worrisome about his research is not that tits at De Hoge Veluwe could be on the verge of a decline but that the decline suggests that many other species are also in danger. "I'm sure if we go to other food chains we'll find the same thing," he states. His findings suggest vulnerabilities to climate change that are universal to all ecosystems. Some scientists say that these weaknesses are best understood using a vocabulary invented in the 1960s by marine biologist David Cushing, formerly the deputy director of the Fisheries Laboratory in Lowestoft, England.

Match and Mismatch

In attempting to explain year-to-year variations in herring stocks, Cushing looked at phytoplankton, the food of the herring larvae. He showed that when the hatching of the herring larvae coincided with phytoplankton blooms, a high proportion of that year's offspring survived to adulthood. This happy state of affairs, which leads to elevated larvae numbers, he called a match. A mismatch, in contrast, is when larvae hatchlings are out of sync with their food, causing a poor year.

The conceptually simple match-mismatch hypothesis is now being applied by a number of researchers to explain the impact of climate warming. The power of the idea comes in part from the fact that a match can refer to different kinds of relationships. For instance, it can describe temporal relationships between predator and prey—as in the case of the tits and the caterpillars—or animal and plant, as in the case of the caterpillars and the oaks. It can be applied to the temporal relationship between different plants. For example, the Fitters found that recent changes in the flowering times of plants are not uniform across species.

Alastair Fitter says that this kind of discrepancy means, among other things, that competition for sunlight, nutrients and water will be altered, with, as he and his father wrote in *Science*, "profound ecosystem and evolutionary consequences." Finally, the match-mismatch concept can be applied to the relation between animals or plants and their physical surroundings. One example is research in Colorado showing that American robins that migrate to high-altitude summer habitats arrive early and wait longer for the winter snow to melt before mating.

Because matches often require synchrony between disparate species, it is no surprise that climate change creates mismatches. Some species are influenced by average temperatures, whereas others respond only to extremes, such as cold snaps.

Tits, oaks and moths, for instance, all seem to respond to temperature in some fashion, though each in a different way. The hatch date for tit eggs appears to be determined about a month earlier, when the eggs are laid. Visser says the birds base the laying date at De Hoge Veluwe on early spring temperatures, which, in contrast to late spring temperatures, have not changed in the past 30 years. Visser has discovered that the hatch date of moth eggs appears to be related to a combination of two factors: the number of winter and early-spring frost days (days when temperatures dip below freezing) and temperatures in late winter and early spring. The winter and early spring temperatures at De Hoge Veluwe have increased in recent decades, although there has been no change in frost days. Finally, the oaks appear to adjust the timing of bud burst depending in part on late spring temperatures, which have risen by two degrees C since 1980. Over thousands of years of evolution, these three organisms have come to synchronize their life cycles using these cues. But climate warming has decoupled the cues so that the old rules do not work anymore.

Long-distance migrants face special challenges. They may need to use cues in one habitat to determine when to depart for another. In the case of migrating birds, arrival at the summer breeding site may require precise timing of departure from wintering grounds.

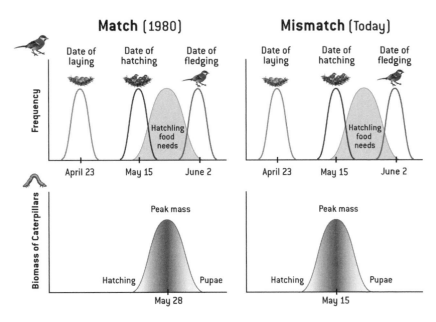

Interdependent species can be "uncoupled" under stress from global warming. In De Hoge Veluwe National Park in the Netherlands, changes in weather patterns have caused oak buds to burst into leaf sooner. As a result, winter moth caterpillars—an important food that great tit chick hatchlings need to reach fledging size—peak in total biomass earlier today (*right*) as compared with two decades ago (*left*). Egg-laying time has not shifted.

But wintering-site cues will not necessarily shift in synchrony with changes in nesting areas, especially if summer and winter sites are separated by thousands of kilometers, as is the case with many birds. One reason is that climate is not changing uniformly across the globe. Compared with temperate regions, for example, the tropics are hardly warming at all. The varied effects of warming on El Niño and other such climate phenomena confuse the picture further. Moreover, because temperatures in the tropics are not strongly correlated with those of temperate regions, many birds do not even use climate cues to decide when to depart tropical wintering sites. Instead they regulate their travels by the length of the day. Of course, global warming has no influence on day length. Thus, such birds are now in danger of arriving at temperate breeding grounds on a date that no longer makes sense.

Christiaan Both of the University of Groningen in the Netherlands says that the pied flycatcher, which migrates 5,000 kilometers from tropical West Africa to De Hoge Veluwe, appears to be suffering from such a mismatch between nesting and wintering-site conditions. Like great tits, the flycatchers feed their hatchlings caterpillars, which reach peak abundance half a month earlier than they did 20 years ago. But the flycatchers are arriving on virtually the same date today as they did in 1980. In a 2001 *Nature* article, Both and his co-author, Marcel Visser, observe that the flycatchers' cue to leave Africa is day length, which explains why the arrival time has not changed. "They have a decision rule that has become maladaptive," Both notes.

The birds have compensated for their late migration by shortening their rest time after they reach the Netherlands. The interval between arrival and breeding has shrunk by 10 days since 1980. But even that is not enough to produce hatchlings in synchrony with the caterpillar peak. Today only the earliest flycatchers have healthy chicks. The rest have underweight offspring, most of which do not return to breed the following year. The birds have stopped nesting in forests with the earliest caterpillar season. Both says that to date, flycatcher numbers do not appear to have dropped off, but that could change if warming continues, because the birds probably cannot reduce the time between arrival and mating any further: "Now they have used up all the safety margin." Both and Visser speculate in *Nature* that the same mechanism that is affecting the pied flycatchers may be one of the factors behind why a number of other European migrants have declined in recent years.

Penguin in a Coal Mine

There are various warning signs but so far few cases in which a mismatch caused by climate change has actually had a serious impact on a plant or animal population. Montana State University ecologist William Fraser, however, says that he has evidence that climate change is causing the extinction of Adélie penguins living on the western coast of the Antarctic Peninsula. Over the past 30 years, Fraser has documented a startling 70 percent decline in the number of Adélie penguins nesting on a number of islands in the vicinity of Palmer Station, one of three U.S. research bases in Antarctica. He believes that climate change is affecting the birds through a mechanism not previously suspected, proving the difficulty of anticipating how nature will respond to warming temperatures.

The Antarctic Peninsula has experienced more warming than almost any other place on the earth.

In the past 50 years, winter temperatures in this part of the Antarctic Peninsula have climbed by almost six degrees C. Counterintuitively, this warming has increased snowfall. That is in part because sea ice, which forms an impermeable cap on the ocean, has decreased with rising temperatures, permitting more moisture to escape into the air. That moisture falls down as snow. Fraser says that colonies sustaining the worst losses are located on the southern slopes of hillsides in the rocky nesting grounds. These areas, he has discovered, are also sustaining the greatest impact from the extra snow falling along the Antarctic Peninsula. Southern slopes, in the lee of the prevailing winds of this region's winter storms, are the last to melt in the spring because they collect snowdrifts in winter and receive relatively little of the sun's warmth (southern slopes are sunniest in the Northern Hemisphere; the opposite is true in the south). But Adélies are "hardwired," Fraser explained in an interview at Palmer Station, "to need the timing of conditions to occur in a very precise chronology," and the extra snow is altering that chronology.

Shortly after they arrive at these islands to breed in October, the birds need bare ground to build their pebble nests. If the snow does not melt in time, they will occasionally try nesting on top of it, but that does not work. When the snow eventually melts, the eggs in such nests become waterlogged, yielding "addled" eggs, not live chicks. Actual precipitation varies from year to year, but over time increased snow has gradually cut the number of new members added to the colonies, which are dying by attrition. Fraser calls the penguins' dilemma a "mismatch between physics and biology." He predicts that as the process continues, more of each island will be affected, extirpating Adélies from the region within 15 years. He says that the Adélies are "extremely sensitive indicators of climate-induced perturbations," suggesting that important changes may be afoot elsewhere. They are "one more piece of evidence that our planet is changing."

Researchers say that in many cases, plants and animals will be able to adapt to changing conditions, avoiding the fate of Fraser's Adélie penguins. Christiaan Both is doing genetic studies of pied flycatchers to see if certain families migrate earlier, raising the possibility that evolution will produce an early migrating sub-species. In at least some instances, however, it is unlikely that an evolutionary trick will be able to solve the problem climate warming has created. For example, it might seem that evolution could produce an early-laying great tit that could remain in synchrony with caterpillars in the oak trees in the De Hoge Veluwe park.

But there is a catch: before adult female tits can produce eggs, they must nourish themselves. They do so by foraging for insects in a different group of trees, primarily larch and birch, which open their leaves before the oaks. These trees have not changed the date of bud burst nearly as much as the oaks have. If this trend continues and if the insects in these trees remain in sync with larch and birch bud burst, the tits could not possibly be ready to breed any earlier in the season.

Many species, such as certain birds and insects, are already responding—and will most likely continue to respond—to global warming by moving their ranges farther north or, in mountainous areas, to higher elevations. Less nimble species, such as trees, will be left behind. Terry L. Root, a biologist at the Center for Environmental Science and Policy at Stanford University, warns that these differential responses will cause existing ecosystems to be "torn apart," leaving altered, more impoverished ones in their place. The problem is compounded by human uses of land, such as cities, farms and highways, which fragment the landscape. Root published a paper in *Nature* last year with evidence of "fingerprints" of global warming on wild plants and animals. She says pollen studies of the end of the last ice age suggest what might happen. Such research shows that as the ice sheet that covered most of North America retreated north, forests were not far behind. But complete communities did not simply move north in synchrony with rising temperatures. Instead the blend of plants and animals changed as the forests moved. Root fears that global warming could produce similar results, creating ecosystems unknown today and casting off species that no longer fit in.

There is, of course, much more research left to do to determine how serious and widespread the problem is. Certain conundrums will also need to be resolved. For example, why are the great tits in the De Hoge

Veluwe park failing to remain in sync with winter moth caterpillars, while birds of the same species at a research site near Cambridge, England, just 400 kilometers away, have altered life cycles in step with the same insects? One thing, says Alastair Fitter, is clear: "The natural world is paying attention to what's going on in the climate." And, he adds, "It's going to get worse."

The Author

Daniel Grossman is a journalist who has been covering environmental topics for 17 years. His recent focus, which has brought him to Greenland and Antarctica in a single year, is global warming and its impact on ecosystems.

Hurricane Katrina, which led to many deaths and billions of dollars worth of damage in Louisiana, Mississippi, and Alabama in 2005, revealed how dangerous sea level changes can be. Since New Orleans is below sea level, it is vulnerable to storm surges from the surrounding Mississippi River and Lake Pontchartrain. As horrific and deadly as Katrina was, the melting of Antarctica's ice sheets could lead to additional disasters worldwide.

The authors of the following article note that if West Antarctica's ice sheet melts completely, it

*could raise sea level by about sixteen feet (five
meters). Many of the world's beaches and coast-
lines would disappear underwater. Islands and
capes already experiencing coastal erosion,
such as many islands in the Caribbean and even
Cape Cod in the United States, could lose miles of
land. Southern Florida, including the city of
Miami, would drown.*

*However, because it is difficult to study the
massive ice sheet, there is little consensus on
exactly how much it is melting and the extent of
the threat to coastal communities. Are coastal
regions doomed if the ice continues to melt? Is
global warming behind the shrinking ice sheet?
The following article addresses these questions
and more. —JV*

"On Thin Ice?"
by Robert A. Bindschadler and Charles R. Bentley
Scientific American, December 2002

Twelve thousand years ago, as the earth emerged from
the last ice age, vast armadas of *Titanic*-size icebergs
invaded the North Atlantic. Purged vigorously from
the enormous ice sheets that smothered half of North
America and Europe at the time, those icebergs displaced
enough water to raise global sea level more than a
meter a year for decades.

As the frozen north melted, the ice gripping the
planet's southernmost continent remained essentially

intact and now represents 90 percent of the earth's solid water. But dozens of scientific studies conducted over the past 30 years have warned that the ice blanketing West Antarctica—the part lying mainly in the Western Hemisphere—could repeat the dramatic acts of its northern cousins. Holding more than three million cubic kilometers of freshwater in its frozen clutches, this ice sheet would raise global sea level five meters (about 16 feet) if it were to disintegrate completely, swamping myriad coastal lowlands and forcing many of their two billion inhabitants to retreat inland.

Most Antarctic scientists have long concurred that the continent's ice has shrunk in the past, contributing to a rise in sea level that continued even after the northern ice sheets were gone. The experts also agree that the ice covering the eastern side of the continent is remarkably stable relative to that in West Antarctica, where critical differences in the underlying terrain make it inherently more erratic. But until quite recently, they disagreed over the likelihood of a catastrophic breakup of the western ice sheet in the near future. Many, including one of us (Bindschadler), worried that streams of ice flowing from the continent's interior toward the Ross Sea might undermine the sheet's integrity, leading to its total collapse in a few centuries or less. Others (including Bentley) pointed to the sheet's recent persistence, concluding that the sheet is reasonably stable.

For a time it seemed the debate might never be resolved. Agreement was hampered by scant data and

Overview/*Antarctic Ice*

- For nearly three decades, numerous Antarctic experts warned that West Antarctica's ice sheet is in the midst of a rapid disintegration that could raise global sea level five meters in a few centuries or less.
- Many of those researchers now think that the ice sheet is shrinking much more slowly than they originally suspected and that sea level is more likely to rise half a meter or less in the next century.
- That consensus is not without its caveats. The ice sheet's poorly understood Amundsen sector now appears to be shrinking faster than previously thought.
- Global warming, which has so far played a negligible role in West Antarctica's fate, is bound to wield greater influence in the future.

the challenge of studying a continent shrouded half the year in frigid darkness. In addition, although areas of the ice sheet have drained quickly in the past, it is difficult to determine whether changes in the size or speed of the ice seen today are a reflection of normal variability or the start of a dangerous trend. In the past few years, though, a variety of field and laboratory studies have yielded a growing consensus on the forces controlling West Antarctica's future, leading experts in both camps to conclude that the ice streams pointing toward the Ross Sea are not currently as threatening as some of us had feared.

We remain puzzled, however, over the ice sheet's ultimate fate. New studies have revealed thinning ice in a long-neglected sector of West Antarctica, suggesting that a destructive process other than ice streams is operating there. And another region—the peninsula that forms Antarctica's northernmost arm—has recently experienced warmer summer temperatures that are almost certainly the reason behind an ongoing breakup of ice along its coasts.

Around the world temperatures have risen gradually since the end of the last ice age, but the trend has accelerated markedly since the mid-1990s with the increase of heat-trapping greenhouse gases in the atmosphere. So far the peninsula seems to be the only part of Antarctica where this recent climate trend has left its mark; average temperatures elsewhere have risen less or even cooled slightly in the past 50 years. Researchers are now scrambling to determine whether global warming is poised to gain a broader foothold at the bottom of the world.

Early Alarms

Indications that the West Antarctic ice sheet might be in the midst of a vanishing act first began cropping up about 30 years ago. In 1974 Johannes Weertman of Northwestern University published one of the most influential early studies, a theoretical analysis of West

Antarctica based on the forces then thought to control the stability of ice sheets. By that time scientists were well aware that most of the land underlying the thick ice in West Antarctica sits far below sea level and once constituted the floor of an ocean. If all the ice were to become liquid, a mountainous landscape would appear, with valleys dipping more than two kilometers below the surface of the sea and peaks climbing two kilometers above it. Because the boundaries of West Antarctica are so sunken, ice at the edges makes extensive contact with the surrounding seawater, and a good deal extends—as floating ice shelves—onto the ocean surface.

Weertman's troubling conclusion was that any ice sheet that fills a marine basin is inherently unstable when global sea level is on the rise, which most scientists agree has been the case for the past 20,000 years. This instability arises because the edges of a marine ice sheet can be easily stressed or even lifted off the underlying sediment by the natural buoyant effects of water. (In contrast, the ice sheet in East Antarctica sits on a continent, most of which rests high above the deleterious influence of the sea.) The outcome of Weertman's simple calculation was that West Antarctica's ice sheet was on a course toward total collapse. Nothing short of a new ice age could alter this fate.

If Weertman's thinking was correct, it meant that the modern ice sheet was already a shrunken version of its former self. Many early discoveries lent support

Chilly Realities

Predicting Antarctic ice sheets' response to changing climate and their influence on sea level is not always straightforward. Here are a few of the less obvious phenomena that scientists must take into account:

Ice need not melt to add to rising seas

Ice that was once on land contributes to global sea level as soon as it begins floating. Indeed, an iceberg most of which sits below the ocean surface—is already displacing as much seawater as it will in liquid form. The same is true for ice shelves, the floating tongues of ice that extend seaward from the edges of continents. In Antarctica, frigid temperatures—averaging about −34 degrees Celsius (−29 degrees Fahrenheit)—mean that very little of that continent's ice ever melts. That might change if global warming becomes more pervasive in the region, but at present Antarctica influences sea level only when solid ice, which is delivered to the coasts by coastal glaciers or by other natural conveyor belts called ice streams, breaks off or adds to existing ice shelves.

Ice can either accelerate or counteract the effects of global warming

Think of a snowy field in the bright sun. Ice and snow reflect much more solar energy back to space than dark oceans and land surfaces do. Such reflection tends to enable an already cold part of the atmosphere above the ice to stay cool, increasing the likelihood that more ice will form.

On the other hand, if global warming heats the atmosphere enough to begin melting the ice and exposing more of the darker surface below, then the region will absorb more solar energy and the air will become warmer still.

Global warming could either slow the rise of sea level or speed it up

Warmer air increases evaporation from the oceans and carries more moisture than cooler air does. So as global warming increases, more evaporated seawater from temperate areas could be transported to polar areas, where it would fall as snow. This process would be further enhanced if global warming were to melt significant amounts of sea ice and expose more of the ocean surface to the atmosphere. All else being equal, ocean water could be preserved as snow faster than it would reenter the sea, alleviating some of the rise in sea level. The catch is that global warming can also cause land ice to melt or break apart more quickly. The ultimate effect of global warming on ice sheets depends on which process dominates.

—R. A. B. and C. R. B.

to this conclusion. Explorers found unusual piles of rock and debris (which only moving ice could have created) on mountain slopes high above the present surface of the ice, indicating that the ice was once much thicker. Likewise, deep gouges carved in the seafloor off the coast implied that the grounded edge of the ice sheet (the part resting on the seafloor) once extended farther out into the ocean. Based on these kinds of limited observations, some researchers estimated that the ice sheet was originally as much as three times its present volume and that it was shrinking fairly slowly—at a rate that would lead to its complete disappearance in another 4,000 to 7,000 years.

The idea that West Antarctica could lurch much more rapidly toward collapse was not formulated until researchers started paying close attention to ice streams—natural conveyor belts hundreds of kilometers long and dozens of kilometers wide. Early investigators inferred that these streams owe their existence in part to tectonic forces that are pulling West Antarctica apart, thinning the crust and allowing an above-average amount of the earth's internal heat to escape. This extra warmth from below could melt the base of the ice sheet, providing a lubricated layer that would allow the ice to move rapidly down even the gentlest of slopes. Indeed, airborne surveys using ice-penetrating radar revealed in the 1970s that two networks of ice streams drain ice from the continent's interior and feed it to West Antarctica's two largest ice shelves, the Ross and the Ronne. As the ice reaches the seaward edge of these shelves, it eventually calves off as huge icebergs. As this dynamic picture of ice streams came to light, so did the first warnings that they harbored the potential to drain the entire ice sheet in a few centuries or less.

Streams of Uncertainty

Driven by the new knowledge that the fate of the West Antarctic ice sheet would depend strongly on how fast these streams were removing ice from the continent, teams from NASA, Ohio State University and the University of Wisconsin-Madison set up summer research camps on and near the ice streams in 1983. Some scientists probed the interior of the streams with radar and seismic explosions; others measured their motion and deformation at the surface. They quickly found that these immense rivers race along at glaciologically breakneck speeds—at hundreds of meters a year, many times faster than the average mountain glacier.

Different field investigators sought explanations for the speed of the streams by melting narrow, kilometer-long holes through the ice to extract samples of the ancient seafloor below. Ground-up shells of marine organisms mixed with pebbles, clay and eroded rock, deposited there over many millennia, now form a bed of muddy paste that is so soft and well lubricated that the ice streams can glide along even more easily than earlier researchers expected. If they had instead found crystalline rock, like that underlying most continental ice sheets, including East Antarctica's, they would have concluded that the greater friction of that material had been inhibiting ice motion.

These realizations left wide open the possibility of swift drainage along the Ross ice streams. In contrast, British workers who were studying the Ronne ice streams on the other side of West Antarctica reassured the world that the prospects were not nearly so grim in their sector. But the scientists camped out near the Ross Ice Shelf had reason to believe that once the Ross ice streams carried away that region's one million cubic kilometers of ice, the rest of the sheet—including the area drained by the Ronne streams and part of the East Antarctic ice sheet—would surely follow.

In the 1990s researchers began to notice another potentially unsettling characteristic of the Ross ice streams: they are not only fast but fickle. Radar examinations of the hidden structure below the surface of the grounded ice revealed that the ice streams were not always in their present locations. Satellite imagery of the Ross Ice Shelf, which is composed of ice that has arrived over the past 1,000 years, discovered crevasses and other features that serve as a natural record of dramatic and unmistakable changes in the streams' rates of flow. Indeed, one stream known simply as "C" apparently stopped flowing suddenly a century and a half ago. Similarly, the Whillans ice stream has been decelerating over the past few decades. If the streams do come and go, as such findings implied, then their future would be much more difficult to predict than once assumed. The most alarming possibility was that the stagnant streams might start flowing again without warning. But reassurance against that prospect, at least for the near future, was soon to come.

About five years ago a slew of reports began providing key evidence that the ice sheet may not have thinned as much as previously estimated. In 2000 Eric J. Steig of the University of Washington used new techniques to analyze an old ice core recovered in 1968 from the heart of West Antarctica. The initial analysis had indicated that the ice was 950 meters higher during the last ice age than it is today, but Steig's improved interpretation reduced that difference to 200 meters. In the mountains of the Executive Committee Range, John O. Stone, another University of Washington researcher, clocked the thinning of the ice sheet by measuring the radioactive by-products of cosmic rays, which have decayed at a known rate since the moment when ice retreat left rock outcrops freshly exposed. These observations put severe limits on the original size of the ice sheet, suggesting that it could have been no more than two and a half times as large as it is today.

By early 2001 scientists on both sides of the debate over the future of West Antarctica's ice sheet were still able to maintain their points of view. Reconciling solid but contradictory evidence required everyone to recognize that great variability on shorter timescales can also appear as lesser variability on longer timescales. Since then, improved measurements of the motion of the Ross ice streams have confirmed that new snowfall is generally keeping pace with ice loss in this sector, meaning that almost no overall shrinkage is occurring at present. And by late 2001 most Antarctic scientists—including both of us—could finally agree that the Ross ice streams are *not* causing the ice to thin at this time. Variations in snowfall versus ice discharge over the past millennium seem to have averaged out—a sign that the ice sheet is less likely to make sudden additions to rising seas than some investigators had expected.

But scientists engaged in this debate know all too well that the dynamic nature of the ice streams dictates that this reconciliation explains only what is going on today. Looking further back in time, for instance, geologic evidence near the U.S. McMurdo Station suggests that the ice sheet retreated through that area very rapidly around 7,000 years ago. Thus, even if not sustained, this type of regional collapse may have occurred during brief periods and could happen again.

To gain a better handle on the future stability of the ice sheet, researchers have also developed a firmer understanding of the forces that control the flow of ice within streams, including an explanation for why the streams can stop, start and change velocity on different timescales. It turns out that sediment (also called till) and water in the seabed are in control over days and years, but global climate, principally through air temperature and sea level, dominates over millennia. This and other new information will make it possible to build more reliable computer models of how the streams might behave centuries hence.

Weak Underbelly Exposed

That the area of the West Antarctic ice sheet drained by the Ross ice streams is in less danger of imminent collapse is good news. But in the past couple of years it has become clear that not all sections of West Antarctica behave in the same way. While field-workers were concentrating their efforts on the ice streams feeding the Ross and Ronne ice shelves, several satellite sensors were patiently collecting data from another sector of the ice sheet, the poorly understood region adjacent to the Amundsen Sea. There groups from the U.S. and Great Britain have discovered that the glaciers in this mysterious area are disappearing at an even faster rate than had been originally hypothesized for the Ross ice streams.

After poring over millions of ice-elevation measurements made from space during the 1980s and 1990s, Duncan J. Wingham of University College London and H. Jay Zwally of the NASA Goddard Space Flight Center showed independently that the parts of the ice sheet that feed the Pine Island and Thwaites glaciers are thinning, the latter at more than 10 centimeters a year. These results mesh beautifully with another recent report, by Eric Rignot of the Jet Propulsion Laboratory in Pasadena, Calif. Using radar interferometry, a technique capable of detecting ice movement as small as a few millimeters, Rignot observed that both glaciers are delivering ice increasingly quickly to the Amundsen Sea *and* shrinking toward the continent's interior. As a result, they currently contribute between 0.1 and 0.2 millimeter a year to global sea-level rise—up to 10 percent of the total. At that rate these glaciers would drain 30 percent of the total ice sheet in 7,500 to 15,000 years, or much faster if a catastrophe like the one hypothesized earlier for the Ross sector were to occur.

This new evidence is no surprise to glaciologists such as Terence J. Hughes of the University of Maine, who long ago dubbed the Amundsen sector "the weak underbelly of the West Antarctic ice sheet." But logistical limitations have discouraged field observations in this remote region for decades—it is far from any permanent research station and is renowned as one of the cloudiest regions on the earth. In addition, unique qualities of the Amundsen Sea glaciers may mean that the hard-won knowledge from the Ross sector will be inapplicable there. The surfaces of the glaciers slope more steeply toward the sea than do the ice streams, for example. And because the glaciers dump their ice directly into the sea instead of adding ice to an existing ice shelf, some scientists have argued that this region may be further along in the disintegration process than any other part of Antarctica.

Turning Up the Heat

Uncertainty over the vulnerability of the Amundsen Sea sector is but one of several unknowns that scientists still must address. Increasing temperatures related to global warming could begin creeping toward the South

Pole from the Antarctic Peninsula, where the summer-time atmosphere has already warmed by more than two degrees C since the 1950s. Even seemingly subtle changes in air temperature could trigger disintegration of ice shelves that are relatively stable at present. Evidence reported this year also suggests that warmer ocean waters mixing from lower latitudes may be melting the ice sheet's grounded edges faster than previously assumed, along with reducing the amount of ice in the Amundsen Sea.

Conveniently for those of us living in the world today, the West Antarctic ice sheet appears to possess more helpful feedbacks—such as those that can cause fast-moving ice streams to stagnate for centuries on end—than either its North American or European cousins long gone. Their destruction occurred suddenly as a result of a few degrees of warming, and yet much of West Antarctica's ice survived. Weertman's early model seems to have oversimplified the ice sheet's own dynamics, which so far have exerted enough control over its size to avoid, or at least forestall, a swift demise.

Based on what we know so far, we predict—albeit cautiously—that the ice sheet will continue shrinking, but only over thousands of years. If that is correct, West Antarctica's average effect on sea level could be roughly double its historic contribution of two millimeters a year. That means this ice sheet would add another meter to sea level only every 500 years. But before anyone breathes a sigh of relief, we must remember that this remarkable ice sheet has been surprising researchers for more than 30 years—and could have more shocks in store.

The Authors

Robert A. Bindschadler and Charles R. Bentley have devoted most of their research careers to investigating the West Antarctic ice sheet and the continent below it. In 23 years at the NASA Goddard Space Flight Center, Bindschadler has led 12 field expeditions to the frozen land down under. Now a senior research fellow at Goddard, he has developed numerous remote-sensing technologies for glaciological application—measuring ice velocity and elevation using satellite imagery and monitoring melting of the ice sheet by microwave emissions, to name just two. Bentley's first visit to West Antarctica lasted 25 months, during which he led an exploratory traverse of the ice sheet as part of the 1957–58 International Geophysical Year expedition. He returned regularly as a member of the geophysics faculty at the University of Wisconsin–Madison until his retirement in 1998.

It seems odd to talk about potential water shortages after a discussion on melting glaciers and rising sea levels, but water shortages could very well be in our future. A growing human population is placing an increased demand on a water supply depleted by drought. Many studies suggest that bodies of freshwater in North America are turning salty and toxic because of runoff that comes primarily from materials used to construct freeways and other roads, not to mention tire residue, gasoline, oil leaks, and other automobile and industrial pollutants. In many countries, the drinkable supply from existing sources has reached critically low levels. In the following article, author Peter Gleick provides a good overview of present and future problems concerning water supplies around the world.

He also mentions a solution to water short-ages that may surprise many readers. In one Namibian city, residents drink treated waste-water, which is mixed with water from rivers, underground aquifers, and other traditional sources. As Gleick suggests, efforts to collect, treat, and then reuse wastewater probably will need to increase to meet the growing demands of businesses, farmers, and individuals. —JV

"Making Every Drop Count"
by Peter H. Gleick
Scientific American, February 2001

The history of human civilization is entwined with the history of the ways we have learned to manipulate water resources. The earliest agricultural communities emerged where crops could be cultivated with dependable rainfall and perennial rivers. Simple irrigation canals permitted greater crop production and longer growing seasons in dry areas. Five thousand years ago settlements in the Indus Valley were built with pipes for water supply and ditches for wastewater. Athens and Pompeii, like most Greco-Roman towns of their time, maintained elaborate systems for water supply and drainage.

As towns gradually expanded, water was brought from increasingly remote sources, leading to sophisticated engineering efforts, such as dams and aqueducts, At the height of the Roman Empire, nine major systems, with an innovative layout of pipes and well-built sewers, supplied the occupants of Rome with as much water per person as is provided in many parts of the industrial world today.

During the industrial revolution and population explosion of the 19th and 20th centuries, the demand for water rose dramatically. Unprecedented construction of tens of thousands of monumental engineering projects designed to control floods, protect clean water supplies, and provide water for irrigation and hydropower brought great benefits to hundreds of millions of people. Thanks to improved sewer systems, water-related diseases such as cholera and typhoid, once endemic throughout the world, have largely been conquered in the more industrial nations. Vast cities, incapable of surviving on their local resources, have bloomed in the desert with water brought from hundreds and even thousands of miles away. Food production has kept pace with soaring populations mainly because of the expansion of artificial irrigation systems that make possible the growth of 40 percent of the world's food. Nearly one fifth of all the electricity generated worldwide is produced by turbines spun by the power of falling water.

Yet there is a dark side to this picture: despite our progress, half of the world's population still suffers with water services inferior to those available to the ancient Greeks and Romans. As the latest United Nations report on access to water reiterated in November of last year, more than one billion people lack access to clean drinking water; some two and a half billion do not have adequate sanitation services. Preventable water-related diseases kill an estimated 10,000 to 20,000 children every day, and the latest evidence suggests that we are falling behind in efforts to solve these problems. Massive cholera outbreaks appeared in the mid-1990s in Latin America, Africa and Asia. Millions of people in Bangladesh and India drink water contaminated with arsenic. And the surging populations throughout the developing world are intensifying the pressures on limited water supplies.

The effects of our water policies extend beyond jeopardizing human health. Tens of millions of people have been forced to move from their homes—often with little warning or compensation—to make way for the reservoirs behind dams. More than 20 percent of all freshwater fish species are now threatened or endangered because dams and water withdrawals have destroyed the free-flowing river ecosystems where they thrive. Certain irrigation practices degrade soil quality and reduce agricultural productivity, heralding a premature end to the green revolution. Groundwater aquifers are being pumped down faster than they are naturally replenished in parts of India, China, the U.S. and elsewhere. And disputes over shared water resources have led to violence and continue to raise local, national and even international tensions [*see box on page 56*].

At the outset of the new millennium, however, the way resource planners think about water is beginning to change. The focus is slowly shifting back to the provision of basic human and environmental needs as the top priority—ensuring "some for all, instead of more for some," as put by Kader Asmal, former minister for water affairs and forestry in South Africa. To accomplish these goals and meet the demands of booming populations, some water experts now call for using existing infrastructure in smarter ways rather than building new facilities, which is increasingly considered the option of last, not first, resort. The challenges we face are to use the water we have more efficiently, to rethink our priorities for water use and to identify alternative supplies of this precious resource.

This shift in philosophy has not been universally accepted, and it comes with strong opposition from some established water organizations. Nevertheless, it may be the only way to address successfully the pressing problems of providing everyone with clean water to drink, adequate water to grow food and a life free from preventable water-related illness. History shows that although access to clean drinking water and sanitation services cannot guarantee the survival of a civilization, civilizations most certainly cannot prosper without them.

Damage from Dams

Over the past 100 years, humankind has designed networks of canals, dams and reservoirs so extensive that the resulting redistribution of freshwater from one place to another and from one season to the next accounts for a small but measurable change in the wobble of the earth as it spins. The statistics are staggering. Before 1900 only 40 reservoirs had been built with storage volumes greater than 25 billion gallons; today almost 3,000 reservoirs larger than this inundate 120 million acres of land and hold more than 1,500 cubic miles of water—as much as Lake Michigan and Lake Ontario combined. The more than 70,000 dams in the U.S. are capable of capturing and storing half of the annual river flow of the entire country.

In many nations, big dams and reservoirs were originally considered vital for national security, economic prosperity and agricultural survival. Until the late 1970s and early 1980s, few people took into account the environmental consequences of these massive projects. Today, however, the results are clear: dams have destroyed the ecosystems in and around countless rivers, lakes and streams. On the Columbia and Snake rivers in the northwestern U.S., 95 percent of the juvenile salmon trying to reach the ocean do not survive passage through the numerous dams and reservoirs that block their way. More than 900 dams on New England and European rivers block Atlantic salmon from their spawning grounds, and their populations have fallen to less than 1 percent of historical levels. Perhaps most infamously, the Aral Sea in central Asia is disappearing because water from the Amu Darya and Syr Darya rivers that once sustained it has been diverted to irrigate cotton. Twenty-four species of fish formerly found only in that sea are currently thought to be extinct.

As environmental awareness has heightened globally, the desire to protect—and even restore—some of these natural resources has grown. The earliest environmental advocacy groups in the U.S. mobilized against dams proposed in places such as Yosemite National Park in California and the Grand Canyon in Arizona. In the 1970s plans in the former Soviet Union to divert the flow of Siberian rivers away from the Arctic stimulated an unprecedented public outcry, helping to halt the projects. In many developing countries, grassroots opposition to the environmental and social costs of big water projects is becoming more and more effective. Villagers and community activists in India have encouraged a public debate over major dams. In China, where open disagreement with government policies is strongly discouraged, protest against the monumental Three Gorges Project has been unusually vocal and persistent.

Until very recently, international financial organizations such as the World Bank, export-import banks and multilateral aid agencies subsidized or paid in full for dams or other water-related civil engineering projects—which often have price tags in the tens of billions of dollars. These organizations are slowly beginning to reduce or eliminate such subsidies, putting more of the financial burden on already strained national economies. Having seen so much ineffective development in the past—and having borne the associated costs (both monetary and otherwise) of that development—many governments are unwilling to pay for new structures to solve water shortages and other problems.

A handful of countries are even taking steps to remove some of the most egregious and damaging dams. For example, in 1998 and 1999 the Maisons-Rouges and Saint-Etienne-du-Vigan dams in the Loire River basin in France were demolished to help restore fisheries in the region. In 1999 the Edwards Dam, which was built in 1837 on the Kennebec River in Maine, was dismantled to open up an 18-mile stretch of the river for fish spawning; within months Atlantic salmon, American shad, river herring, striped bass, shortnose sturgeon, Atlantic sturgeon, rainbow smelt and American eel had returned to the upper parts of the river. Altogether around 500 old, dangerous or

Where the Water Will Be in 2025

The total amount of water withdrawn globally from rivers, underground aquifers and other sources has increased nine-fold since 1900 (*chart*). Water use per person has only doubled in that time, however, and it has even declined slightly in recent years. Despite this positive trend, some experts worry that improvements in water-use efficiency will fail to keep pace with projected population growth. Estimated annual water availability per person in 2025 reveals that at least 40 percent of the world's 7.2 billion people may face serious problems with agriculture, industry or human health if they must rely solely on natural endowments of freshwater. Severe water shortages could also strike particular regions of water-rich countries, such as the U.S. and China.

People's access to water also depends on factors not reflected here, such as political and economic conditions, changing climate patterns and available technology.

—*P. H. G.*

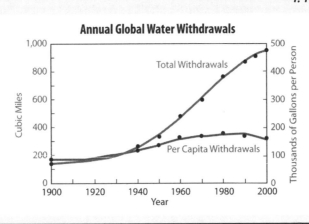

Annual Global Water Withdrawals

environmentally harmful dams have been removed from U.S. rivers in the past few years.

Fortunately—and unexpectedly—the demand for water is not rising as rapidly as some predicted. As a result, the pressure to build new water infrastructures has diminished over the past two decades. Although population, industrial output and economic productivity have continued to soar in developed nations, the rate at which people withdraw water from aquifers, rivers and lakes has slowed. And in a few parts of the world, demand has actually fallen.

Demand Is Down—But for How Long?

What explains this remarkable turn of events? Two factors: people have figured out how to use water more efficiently, and communities are rethinking their priorities for water use. Throughout the first three quarters of the 20th century, the quantity of freshwater consumed per person doubled on average; in the U.S., water withdrawals increased 10-fold while the population quadrupled. But since 1980 the amount of water consumed per person has actually decreased, thanks to a range of new technologies that help to conserve water in homes and industry. In 1965, for instance, Japan used approximately 13 million gallons of water to produce $1 million of commercial output; by 1989 this had dropped to 3.5 million gallons (even accounting for inflation)—almost a quadrupling of water productivity. In the U.S., water withdrawals have fallen by more than 20 percent from their peak in 1980.

As the world's population continues to grow, dams, aqueducts and other kinds of infrastructure will still have to be built, particularly in developing countries where basic human needs have not been met. But such projects must be built to higher standards and with more accountability to local people and their environment than in the past. And even in regions where new projects seem warranted, we must find ways to meet demands with fewer resources, minimum ecological disruption and less money.

The fastest and cheapest solution is to expand the productive and efficient use of water. In many countries, 30 percent or more of the domestic water supply never reaches its intended destinations, disappearing from leaky pipes, faulty equipment or poorly maintained distribution systems. The quantity of water that Mexico City's supply system loses is enough to meet the needs of a city the size of Rome, according to recent estimates. Even in more modern systems, losses of 10 to 20 percent are common.

When water does reach consumers, it is often used wastefully. In homes, most water is literally flushed away. Before 1990 most toilets in the U.S. drew about six gallons of water for each flush. In 1992 the U.S. Congress passed a national standard mandating that all new residential toilets be low-flow models that require only 1.6 gallons per flush—a 70 percent improvement with a single change in technology. It will take time to replace all older toilets with the newer, better ones. A number of cities, however, have found the water conservation made possible by the new technology to be so significant—and the cost of saving that water to be so low—that they have established programs to speed up the transition to low-flow toilets.

Even in the developing world, technologies such as more efficient toilets have a role to play. Because of the difficulty of finding new water sources for Mexico City, city officials launched a water conservation program that involved replacing 350,000 old toilets. The replacements have already saved enough water to supply an additional 250,000 residents. And numerous other options for both industrial and non-industrial nations are available as well, including better leak detection, less wasteful washing machines, drip irrigation and water-conserving plants in outdoor landscaping.

The amount of water needed for industrial applications depends on two factors: the mix of goods and services demanded by society and the processes chosen to generate them. For instance, producing a ton of steel before World War II required 60 to 100 tons of water. Current technology can make a ton of steel with less than six tons of water. Replacing old technology with new techniques reduces water needs by a factor of 10. Producing a ton of aluminum, however, requires only one and a half tons of water. Replacing the use of steel with aluminum, as has been happening for years in the automobile industry, can further lower water use. And telecommuting from home can save the hundreds of gallons of water required to produce, deliver and sell a

Continuing Conflict over Freshwater

Myths, legends and written histories reveal repeated controversy over freshwater resources since ancient times. Scrolls from Mesopotamia, for instance, indicate that the states of Umma and Lagash in the Middle East clashed over the control of irrigation canals some 4,500 years ago.

Throughout history, water has been used as a military and political goal, as a weapon of war and even as a military target. But disagreements most often arise from the fact that water resources are not neatly partitioned by the arbitrary political borders set by governments. Today nearly half of the land area of the world lies within international river basins, and the watersheds of 261 major rivers are shared by two or more countries. Overlapping claims to water resources have often provoked disputes, and in recent years local and regional conflicts have escalated over inequitable allocation and use of water resources.

A small sampling of water conflicts that occurred in the 20th century demonstrates that treaties and other international diplomacy can sometimes encourage opposing countries to cooperate—but not always before blood is shed. The risk of future strife cannot be ignored: disputes over water will become more common over the next several decades as competition for this scarce resource intensifies. —*P .H. G.*

U.S.: 1924

Local farmers dynamite the Los Angeles aqueduct several times in an attempt to prevent diversions of water from the Owens Valley to Los Angeles.

India and Pakistan: 1947 to 1960

Partitioning of British India awkwardly divides the waters of the Indus River valley between India and Pakistan. Competition over irrigation supplies incites numerous conflicts between the two nations; in one case, India stems the flow of water into Pakistani irrigation canals. After 12 years of World Bank–led negotiations, a 1960 treaty helps to resolve the discord.

Egypt and Sudan: 1958

Egypt sends troops into contested territory between the two nations during sensitive negotiations concerning regional politics and water from the Nile. Signing of a Nile waters treaty in 1959 eases tensions.

Israel, Jordan and Syria: 1960s and 1970s

Clashes over allocation, control and diversion of the Yarmouk and Jordan rivers continue to the present day.

South Africa: 1990

A pro-apartheid council cuts off water to 50,000 black residents of Wesselton Township after protests against wretched sanitation and living conditions.

continued on following page

continued from previous page

Iraq: 1991

During the Persian Gulf War, Iraq destroys desalination plants in Kuwait. A United Nations coalition considers using the Ataturk Dam in Turkey to shut off the water flow of the Euphrates River to Iraq.

India: 1991 to present

An estimated 50 people die in violence that continues to erupt between the Indian states of Karnataka and Tamil Nadu over the allocation of irrigation water from the Cauvery River, which flows from one state into the other.

Yugoslavia: 1999

NATO shuts down water supplies in Belgrade and bombs bridges on the Danube River, disrupting navigation.

gallon of gasoline, even accounting for the water required to manufacture our computers.

The largest single consumer of water is agriculture—and this use is largely inefficient. Water is lost as it is distributed to farmers and applied to crops. Consequently, as much as half of all water diverted for agriculture never yields any food. Thus, even modest improvements in agricultural efficiency could free up huge quantities of water. Growing tomatoes with traditional irrigation systems may require 40 percent more water than growing tomatoes with drip systems. Even our diets have an effect on our overall water needs. Growing a pound of corn can take between 100 and 250 gallons of water, depending on soil and climate conditions and irrigation methods. But growing the grain to produce a pound of beef can require between 2,000 and 8,500 gallons. We can conserve water not only by altering how we choose to grow our food but also by changing what we choose to eat.

Shifting where people use water can also lead to tremendous gains in efficiency. Supporting 100,000 high-tech California jobs requires some 250 million gallons of water a year; the same amount of water used in the agricultural sector sustains fewer than 10 jobs— a stunning difference. Similar figures apply in many other countries. Ultimately these disparities will lead to more and more pressure to transfer water from agricultural uses to other economic sectors. Unless the agricultural community embraces water conservation efforts, conflicts between farmers and urban water users will worsen.

The idea that a planet with a surface covered mostly by water could be facing a water shortage seems incredible. Yet 97 percent of the world's water is too salty for human consumption or crops, and much of the rest is out of reach in deep groundwater or in glaciers and ice caps. Not surprisingly, researchers have investigated techniques for dipping into the immense supply of water in the oceans. The technology to desalinate brackish water or saltwater is well developed, but it remains expensive and is currently an option only in wealthy but dry areas near the coast. Some regions, such as the Arabian Gulf, are highly dependent on desalination, but the process remains a minor contributor to overall water supplies, providing less than 0.2 percent of global withdrawals.

With the process of converting saltwater to freshwater so expensive, some companies have turned to another possibility: moving clean water in ships or even giant plastic bags from regions with an abundance of the resource to those places around the globe suffering from a lack of water. But this approach, too, may have serious economic and political constraints.

Rather than seeking new distant sources of water, smart planners are beginning to explore using alternative *kinds* of water to meet certain needs. Why should communities raise all water to drinkable standards and then use that expensive resource for flushing toilets or watering lawns? Most water ends up flowing down the drain after a single use, and developed countries spend billions of dollars to collect and treat this wastewater before dumping it into a river or the ocean. Meanwhile, in poorer countries, this water is often simply returned untreated to a river or lake where it may pose a threat to human health or the environment. Recently attention has begun to focus on reclaiming and reusing this water.

Wastewater can be treated to different levels suitable for use in a variety of applications, such as recharging groundwater aquifers, supplying industrial processes, irrigating certain crops or even augmenting potable supplies. In Windhoek, Namibia, for instance, residents have used treated wastewater since 1968 to supplement the city's potable water supply; in drought years, such water has constituted up to 30 percent of Windhoek's drinking water supply. Seventy percent of Israeli municipal wastewater is treated and reused, mainly for agricultural irrigation of nonfood crops. Efforts to capture, treat and reuse more wastewater are also under way in neighboring Jordan. By the mid-1990s residents of California relied on more than 160 billion gallons of reclaimed water annually for irrigating landscapes, golf courses and crops, recharging ground-water aquifers, supplying industrial processes and even flushing toilets.

New approaches to meeting water needs will not be easy to implement: economic and institutional structures still encourage the wasting of water and the destruction of ecosystems. Among the barriers to better water planning and use are inappropriately low water prices, inadequate information on new efficiency technologies, inequitable water allocations, and government subsidies for growing water-intensive crops in arid regions or building dams.

Part of the difficulty, however, also lies in the prevalence of old ideas among water planners. Addressing the world's basic water problems requires fundamental changes in how we think about water, and such changes are coming about slowly. Rather than trying endlessly to find enough water to meet hazy projections of future desires, it is time to find a way to meet our present and future needs with the water that is already available, while preserving the ecological cycles that are so integral to human well-being.

The Author

Peter H. Gleick is director of the Pacific Institute for Studies in Development, Environment and Security, a nonprofit policy research think tank based in Oakland, Calif. Gleick co-founded the institute in 1987. He is considered one of the world's leading experts on freshwater problems, including sustainable use of water, water as it relates to climate change, and conflicts over shared water resources.

2 Threatened Species and Ecosystems

Lemurs are our distant primate cousins. It is hard to see the link, as lemurs are small, furry creatures with big eyes. They seem to look nothing like humans, but such is the power of evolution. Researchers are only just now beginning to understand how lemurs first emerged and how they all wound up in Madagascar, an island off the eastern coast of Africa. The latest studies suggest that lemurs first appeared 37 to 40 million years ago in Africa before they crossed the Mozambique Channel and colonized Madagascar.

Any time a species is limited to one area, it is at risk because disease, natural disasters, and environmental changes could wipe out the whole species. Sadly, humans are the greatest threat to lemurs in the wild. At least seventeen species of lemur have become extinct in the recent past, and many more extinctions likely preceded these. Of the forty-nine existing lemur species, most are categorized as being critically endangered, endangered, or vulnerable. Better management of forests and other lemur habitat regions in

Madagascar could help to save our primate cousins. Aside from maintaining wildlife diversity, preservation of these animals would ensure that scientists could further study lemurs to tell us more about the evolution of our own species. —JV

"Madagascar's Lemurs"
by Ian Tattersall
Scientific American, **January 1993**

From dense rain forests to broad coastal plains, from deciduous thickets to desert, Madagascar offers an extraordinary range of environments. These habitats harbor an equally extraordinary primate fauna that shows more clearly than any other what our own primate ancestors were like early in the Age of Mammals, approximately 50 million years ago.

These animals are the lemurs, Madagascar's dominant mammals. Why they are there is not entirely clear. The story used to be that the 1,000-mile-long Madagascan minicontinent had simply preserved (in somewhat impoverished fashion) an archaic fauna that was marooned on it when Madagascar separated from the African mainland and drifted out to sea. In many ways the island's living "lower" primates more closely resemble the primates of the Eocene epoch (about 57 to 35 million years ago) than they do the "higher" primates dominating the tropical continents today. That fact was taken to imply that the separation had occurred in the Eocene or thereabouts.

But we now know that Madagascar began its journey away from Africa as much as 165 million years ago, when the dinosaurs ruled and the only mammals were tiny and vaguely shrewlike. Moreover, the island appears to have reached its present separation of roughly 250 miles from Africa some tens of millions of years before the great diversification of the mammals and thus well before today's familiar groups such as the primates, bats and rodents came into existence.

For land-bound latecomers such as primates, then, the only possible means of access to Madagascar was by "rafting": floating across the Mozambique Channel from Africa on matted tangles of vegetation. Arriving thus, the ancestral lemurs would have found an incredible wealth of ecological opportunities on an island that is only slightly smaller than Texas and topographically, climatically and ecologically much more diverse.

The island of Madagascar looks rather like a giant left footprint in the sea, its long axis oriented more or less north-south. It extends from within 12 degrees of the equator all the way to the southern subtropical zone. Its eastern side presents a steep escarpment to the prevailing easterly winds; here heavy rainfall year-round supports a dense growth of rain forest. To the west, a rugged central plateau slopes more gently to broad coastal plains that become drier toward the south. Moist forests in the northwest give way to deciduous forests and thickets. These in turn yield in the far south to an extraordinary desert-adapted flora in which as many as 98 percent of the species are unique. Add to these major regions a host of local microclimates and secondary physiographic features, and you have an unparalleled assortment of environments for forest-living mammals to exploit.

No one knows what the range of habitats was in Madagascar at the remote time when primates first arrived or what lived in those habitats; the fossil record is simply lacking. What is certain, though, is that the primates flourished and that by the time human beings arrived under 2,000 years ago the island was home to at least 45 lemur species. These primates ranged in body size from the two-ounce mouse lemur, *Microcebus*, to the 400-pound *Archaeoindris*, a match for a large gorilla.

Each of the lemur species was a lower primate, belonging (with the bush babies, pottos and lorises) to the primate suborder Strepsirhini. We, on the other hand, are higher primates, belonging (with the monkeys and apes) to the suborder Anthropoidea. (There is no consensus about which group the tiny and enigmatic tarsier of Southeast Asia belongs to.) The distinction between lower and higher primates is in fact a rather archaic concept that is now going out of fashion, but it is a convenient one to use here.

The higher primates appeared on the evolutionary scene much later than did the lower primates, from one of which they presumably evolved toward the end of the Eocene. Madagascar's lemurs and their continental cousins have much in common with Eocene forms, retaining a suite of physical characteristics that have been lost among higher primates. But only in Madagascar do we still find lower primates that are diurnal, or active during the day. Virtually all modern higher primates are diurnal, and if anything in paleontology is certain, it is that all anthropoids are descended from a diurnal common ancestor. So if we wish to find analogies to our remote Eocene ancestors, we must turn to the primates of Madagascar.

Modern lower and higher primates are distinguished from one another by a number of structural features, most significantly in their nervous systems and sense organs. The lower primates have much smaller brains relative to body size than do higher primates. They also differ in the development of the association areas, which govern the transfer of information between the various brain centers.

The balance between the senses of vision and smell also differs. Although the eyes of lower primates are quite forward-facing, the left and right visual fields do not overlap as much as they do in higher primates. This arrangement limits depth perception to the central part of the field of view. And whereas it is natural that the nocturnal lower primates lack color-sensitive cone cells in their retinas, what little is known about visual discrimination in the diurnal lemurs suggests that their color vision is at best limited.

As for the sense of smell, the lower primates have roomier nasal cavities than do higher primates, with more complex internal structures. Living lower primates retain the primitive mammalian rhinarium, or "wet nose." It is part of a system for the transfer of particles to the nasal cavity, where they are analyzed by an organ that is, at most, vestigial in most higher primates.

Many lower primates (but only a few South American monkeys among the higher primates) have scent glands that exude substances used to "mark" the environment. This process is important in communication between individuals. Visual cues are less important; the faces of lower primates lack the musculature needed to produce the complex expressions through which higher primates convey their states of mind.

Living primates in general have lost the primitive claws that enabled the first pre-Eocene primates to scale trees without the ability to grasp. In their stead is a thumb, shifted away from the other digits, that is at least to some extent opposable to them, and sensitive tactile pads on the fingertips, which are backed by flat nails. This fundamental change has consequences that extend far beyond locomotion as well as into manipulative abilities. But whereas higher primates generally manipulate objects using the thumb in opposition to the other digits, lemurs tend to pick things up with the whole hand. An item held in this way is then more likely to be sniffed rather than inspected visually and turned in the fingers for further examination.

Both the lower and the higher primates are, of course, extremely diverse groups, whose members represent myriad variations on the themes outlined above. Nevertheless, the lower primates are obviously more primitive than the higher primates (with respect to the body systems discussed) in the sense that they more closely resemble the ancestor from which both modern groups emerged. Although fossils are limited to bones and teeth, they reveal clearly that in the Eocene primate brains were even smaller in relation to body size than are those typical of modern lemurs and that the visual sense had not achieved the total domination over olfaction we see in today's higher primates. Eocene primate hands and feet were certainly capable of grasping but could probably manipulate objects no more precisely than lemurs do at present. In other words, as functioning organisms, Eocene primates were probably not too different from today's lemurs. They were certainly close enough so that by studying the lives of lemurs we can glimpse something of the Eocene behavioral potential from which our vaunted human capacities ultimately arose.

Not until the 1960s did information about the behavior of lemurs begin to be available from field studies in Madagascar. The results of those studies have been increasingly at odds with earlier anticipations. For example, as long as it was possible to think of "the lemur" as a general ancestral model, the expectation, if any, was simple: lemurs would show a set of relatively stereotypical behavior patterns, similar to those exhibited by early primates and from which the higher primates had managed to emancipate themselves. Yet perhaps the most remarkable revelation of the field studies is how diverse the lemurs are in their ways of life.

Of course, certain predictions from anatomy were indeed borne out. Olfactory marking, using urine and feces as well as the secretions of specialized glands, has been shown to be a significant component of lemur behavior. To judge by its wide occurrence among mammals, such marking is an ancient behavior, and few would question its importance in communication among Eocene primates.

Lemurs also turn out, as expected, to have a tendency to explore their environments with their noses—to choose ripe fruit, for example, by smell rather than by appearance. Undoubtedly, then, olfaction is of the greatest importance to members of all five living families of lemurs, as it was to their Eocene precursors, and much more so than it is to most higher primates. But does the reverse apply to vision? Anyone who has watched a sifaka lemur hurtle through the forest would conclude that the animal is hardly handicapped by its lack of a higher primate's visual system.

Lemurs, in fact, turn out to be as diverse as or even more so than the higher primates in most aspects of their behavior and ecology. Their diets, for instance, consist of much the same items as those consumed by the higher primates: fruit, flowers, leaves, buds and insects. But feeding on nectar, which is unusual in higher primates, is being increasingly noted. As a whole, lemurs tend to be dietary generalists, but some at least are highly specialized—for example, the bamboo lemurs. Many of them concentrate not just on bamboo but on particular parts of bamboo plants. Indeed, individuals of the species *Hapalemur aureus*, weighing only a couple of pounds each, daily eat shoots containing enough cyanide to kill half a dozen humans.

Similarly, lemurs occupy nearly all of the vegetational habitats exploited by higher primates, from rain forest to arid brush. Again, whereas almost all higher primates are diurnal, some lemurs are nocturnal, others diurnal and yet others "cathemeral," spreading their activity fairly evenly between daylight and darkness.

The range of types of social organization among lemurs is enormous. Some lead more or less solitary lives, in which small female ranges are overlapped by larger male ones. In certain species, adult pairs rear immature offspring, whereas in others, small groups consist of just a few adults of each sex. And still other species live in fluid groups or in more stable larger units that contain a couple of dozen individuals or more.

Within these broad categories, there are still further variations. What is perhaps most surprising is that even within the same species, substantial variation in social organization may be found from place to place. What seems to be most significant is that even though lemur brains tend to be smaller than those of higher primates, at least some lemurs display the complex sociality we usually associate with the higher primates.

The picture that is therefore beginning to emerge of the behavioral variety of the lemurs has important implications for the understanding of our own Eocene ancestors. Despite the retention of such primitive behavioral traits as olfactory marking, the wide variety suggests that from the beginning, well before the increase in brain size that we associate with the higher primates today, primates showed a behavioral flexibility and adaptability that belie the inference most people would draw from the description of these early forms as "primitive." It seems to me that this is the essential evolutionary heritage of our order, something far more important than any of the anatomic characteristics to which we are wont to draw attention. As higher primates ourselves, we tend to look at the lemurs and ask why they did not evolve further in our direction. But in doing this, we are missing the critical point that, as a whole, the lemurs have actually inherited from their Eocene ancestors, as we have from ours, the most significant primate characteristic of all.

Looking at this picture from another perspective, it is certainly clear that the lemurs had no need of higher primate physical characteristics to make full use of the varied ecological opportunities that Madagascar offered them. Perhaps this point is emphasized most dramatically by considering the full range of lemur species that existed on Madagascar when humans first arrived there. The present range is impressive enough: at the small end is the tiny two-ounce mouse lemur and at the large end, the 15-pound babakoto. But in its pristine state, the island was home to a spectrum of primate types that equals, if it does not surpass, the entire variety achieved by anthropoids in the rest of the world.

Late in the 19th century, excavations at sites in the central plateau of Madagascar began bringing to light the subfossil, or partially fossilized, remains of large-bodied extinct lemurs that were clearly not of great age. We know of at least 15 species of subfossil lemurs, belonging to eight or possibly more different genera. All of them are larger than any surviving lemurs. The same pattern of large body size is found among the nonprimate members of the subfossil fauna, including the "elephant bird," *Aepyornis maximus* (the largest bird that ever lived, possibly weighing almost half a ton), the pygmy hippopotamus and a giant tortoise.

A long series of studies has revealed an astonishing array of locomotor and positional behaviors among the subfossil lemurs. Even by themselves, the living lemurs show a great variety of such behaviors, ranging from the rapid, scurrying quadrupedal motion of the tiny *Microcebus* to the spectacular leaping of the long-legged indrid lemurs (sifakas, babakotos and the like). It cannot really be said that any of the living lemurs is excluded from any part of the forest environment by its anatomic locomotor specializations, but it is generally true that most species avoid spending much time on the ground. The only notable exception is the ringtailed lemur, *Lemur catta*.

Among the extinct lemurs, on the other hand, was a group that was clearly adapted for life on the ground. This is the family Archaeolemuridae, containing the two medium-sized genera *Archaeolemur* and *Hadropithecus*. Laurie R. Godfrey of the University of Massachusetts at Amherst (the source for all the estimates of subfossil body weight presented here) has estimated that the various archaeolemurid species weighed between 35 and 55 pounds.

These lemurs were rather powerfully built, short-legged relatives of the indrids, with highly specialized teeth. Clifford J. Jolly of New York University has compared them, respectively, with two African higher primates, the common and gelada baboons. The common baboon is an extremely adaptable form, at home in woodlands and deciduous forests as well as in the savanna habitats in which it is so familiar. The gelada baboon is specifically adapted to the treeless Ethiopian highlands, and virtually all its food is derived from terrestrial sources. Both the dentition and what is known of the body skeleton of *Hadropithecus* suggest strongly that this lemur had similar dietary and habitat preferences.

Another extinct indrid relative showed a totally different set of adaptations. For analogues, one must look well beyond the primates. *Palaeopropithecus* comprised at least two species with a weight range of perhaps 90 to 130 pounds. Ross MacPhee, my colleague at the American Museum of Natural History, has analyzed a substantially complete skeleton recovered in northern Madagascar a few years ago and concluded it was a generally slow-moving and somewhat slothlike arboreal hanger, built for flexibility rather than strength. Its even larger relative *Archaeoindris* (probably more than 400 pounds) is poorly known, but Martine

Vuillaume-Randriamanantena of the University of Madagascar believes it was probably a terrestrial quadruped somewhat like the extinct ground sloths of the New World. Both of these forms had specializations of the skull, particularly of the nose area, that are unmatched among living primates.

Extinct lemurs include *Archaeolemur* (*two are shown at bottom*), *Megaladapis* (*upper left*) and *Palaeopropithecus* (*upper right*). *Archaeolemur* was about the size of a female baboon and was adapted to life on the ground. In contrast, *Megaladapis*, weighing as much as 170 pounds, was arboreal and seems to have had adaptations similar to those of the Australian koala. *Palaeopropithecus*, which weighed at most 130 pounds, was a slothlike arboreal dweller. These reconstructions—done with the advice of Laurie R. Godfrey of the University of Massachusetts at Amherst—are based on fossils that have been unearthed since the late 19th century. Excavations have provided mostly incomplete skeletons of at least 15 species of extinct lemurs, belonging to some eight genera.

We also have to look outside our own order to
find an analogue to the best-known subfossil lemur,
Megaladapis. The three species, ranging in weight from
about 90 to 170 pounds, have been described by Alan
C. Walker of the Johns Hopkins School of Medicine as
closest in locomotion to the marsupial koala of Australia.
Like the koala, these lemurs would have climbed slowly,
presumably preferring vertical supports, and they had
limited leaping capabilities. A number of specializations
of the skull may have compensated for such locomotor
limitations. They would have allowed the animal to
feed in a large radius from a single sitting position.

The best known of the sites that have yielded
extinct lemurs is Ampasambazimba in Madagascar's
central highlands. The 14 primate species (including
both extinct and surviving lemurs) whose bones have
been recovered there compare favorably in abundance
with the species at any other place in the world where
primates are found. Yet Ampasambazimba is in the
middle of what is now an essentially treeless plateau.
How does it boast this rich and heterogeneous forest-
living fauna?

Studies dating from early in this century seemed to have
the answer. Before the advent of humans, the argument
goes, Madagascar was essentially fully forested. The fact
that forest had survived only in patches was attributed
to the propensity of the early settlers to burn off vast
areas of forest to provide grazing for cattle and land for
agriculture. Indeed, the process is still only too evident.

Following this argument, loss of habitat must have been at least a major influence in the disappearance of Madagascar's large birds and mammals. There was also a selective aspect of this extinction: the lemurs known to have become extinct were large bodied and thus of the greatest interest and vulnerability to hunters. Presumably, they also reproduced more slowly than the smaller forms that have survived. The case for a combination of direct and indirect human activity as the agent of extinction seems compelling.

Climatic change has also been promoted as an agent of extinction, initially because many subfossil sites consist of dried-up lakes or marshes. As a total explanation of the extinctions, drying was never completely convincing. Still, interest in a possible climatic effect has been revived recently by the demonstration that some of the grasslands of Madagascar's center are of long (and certainly prehuman) standing.

Analyses of lake cores by David A. Burney of Fordham University have underscored the fact that, like every other region of the earth, Madagascar has undergone climatic fluctuations over the past few thousand years. At the end of the last ice age some 10,000 years ago, Madagascar's forests were apparently just beginning to recover from a period of contraction. It is therefore hardly surprising that the central highlands were not fully forested by the time Madagascar's first people arrived.

Climatic stress and the consequent reduction and redistribution of forests thus constitute one potential

factor in the disappearance of the subfossil fauna of
Madagascar. But it is clear that in that land as elsewhere,
periodic disturbances of this kind have occurred
throughout time. The ancestral lineages of the extinct
lemurs obviously survived these earlier vicissitudes, and
there is no reason to believe that on their own the most
recent (rather mild) round of climate changes should
have had a fatal effect on several lineages simultaneously.
This is especially true when we consider that most
subfossil lemurs were probably ecological generalists.
Megaladapis, *Palaeopropithecus* and *Archaeolemur*,
among others, lived in environments ranging from
humid to arid and were clearly highly adaptable in
terms of choice of habitat. Hence, something other
than simply another cycle of disturbance of natural
habitat must be invoked to explain the disappearance
of the giant lemurs. Only one truly novel factor presents
itself: *Homo sapiens*.

To talk of the "extinction event" of the large-bodied
lemurs implies a process that has ended. That is not so.
The extinct and living lemurs form part of a single
process that is continuing. The smaller, fleeter lemurs
have survived so far, but they are themselves under
increasing pressure from an expanding human population. The toll of hunting increases as human numbers
and the use of more sophisticated weapons do. Another
important consideration is the population movements
that tend to erode the local beliefs that, in certain places,
have traditionally protected various lemur species.

More worrying yet is destruction of habitat, principally by slash-and-burn agriculture but also by the cutting of trees for fuel and by commercial logging. The largest continuous forest tract in Madagascar lies along the island's humid eastern escarpment. By analyzing historical documents and satellite images, Glen M. Green and Robert W. Sussman of Washington University have shown that 66 percent of the area covered by this forest at the turn of the century had been denuded by 1985. They estimate that within another 35 years only the steepest slopes of the escarpment will still bear trees. In the flatter western and southern regions of the island, the rate of disappearance of forest is probably faster.

Such pressures have existed for many decades. In the 1920s the colonial authorities in Madagascar set up one of the world's first systems of natural reserves. But as one of the world's poorest countries, Madagascar, despite its government's genuine concern, cannot afford to police these reserves adequately or, in some cases, at all. Fortunately, in recent years the island has attracted the attention of the international conservation community. The country figured recently in one of the first "debt for nature" swaps, in which foreign debt is reduced in exchange for the protection of natural areas.

It is, of course, the real and immediate needs of desperately poor local communities that are being met by most of the forest destruction. In many cases, large-scale agreements on conservation have yet to devolve from the higher governmental sphere to actual projects on the ground. But as they do, one can hope for the stabilization and perhaps even for the long-term improvement of Madagascar's environmental situation.

Meanwhile the lemur populations continue to dwindle. It is tragic to see any part of the world's biodiversity disappear, but the tragedy is particularly acute in the case of Madagascar's lemurs, which still have so much to teach us about our own past.

The Author

Ian Tattersall is a paleontologist and primatologist who has worked extensively on the living and subfossil lemurs of Madagascar as well as on a range of problems in early primate and human evolution. Curator in the department of anthropology of the American Museum of Natural History, Tattersall is especially interested in the integration of evolutionary theory with the fossil record. He has also served as curator for several major exhibitions at the museum, including the highly acclaimed Hall of Human Biology and Evolution in 1993 and Madagascar: Island of the Ancestors in 1989.

We sometimes take it for granted that super-markets will carry a variety of seafood for consumers, or that family fishing trips will yield a catch or two. If current trends continue, however, fish and other seafood may be in short supply. In the following article, author Carl Safina explains how wild fish are no match for modern fishing methods. High-tech tools such as radar, satellites, and sonar direct large ships to the exact spots where fish gather and breed. Even worse, the giant nets fishermen use cannot distinguish between the desired catch and other sea creatures, so everything from endangered sea turtles to dolphins and other marine mammals can become ensnared in them.

The article also brings up an interesting point about aquaculture. Fish farming would seem to be the perfect solution to overfishing, but it, too, poses environmental threats. For example, fish farms often necessitate the construction of pens adjacent to the coast. To make room for the pens, woody trees or shrubs that grow in these coastal regions are frequently cut down. Since the roots of these salt-tolerant trees provide habitat and refuge for shrimp and fish in the wild, such fish farms can hurt some wild populations. One solution is to buy only fish raised in proper, environmentally sound conditions. California's Monterey Bay Aquarium publishes recommendations for consumers at its Seafood Watch Web site (http://www.mbayaq.org/cr/seafoodwatch.asp). —JV

"The World's Imperiled Fish"
by Carl Safina
Scientific American Presents: The Oceans, **1998**

The 19th-century naturalist Jean-Baptiste de Lamarck is well known for his theory of the inheritance of acquired characteristics, but he is less remembered for his views on marine fisheries. In pondering the subject, he wrote, "Animals living in . . . the sea waters . . . are protected from the destruction of their species by man. Their multiplication is so rapid and their means of evading pursuit or traps are so great, that there is no likelihood of his being able to destroy the entire species of any of these animals." Lamarck was also wrong about evolution.

One can forgive Lamarck for his inability to imagine that humans might catch fish faster than these creatures could reproduce. But many people—including those in professions focused entirely on fisheries—have committed the same error of thinking. Their mistakes have reduced numerous fish populations to extremely low levels, destabilized marine ecosystems and impoverished many coastal communities. Ironically, the drive for short-term profits has cost billions of dollars to businesses and taxpayers, and it has threatened the food security of developing countries around the world. The fundamental folly underlying the current decline has been a widespread failure to recognize that fish are wildlife—the only wildlife still hunted on a large scale.

Because wild fish regenerate at rates determined by nature, attempts to increase their supply to the marketplace must eventually run into limits. That threshold seems to have been passed in all parts of the Atlantic, Mediterranean and Pacific: these regions each show dwindling catches. Worldwide, the extraction of wild fish has seemingly stagnated at about 84 million metric tons.

In some areas where the catches peaked as long ago as the early 1970s, landings have since decreased by more than 50 percent. Even more disturbingly, some of the world's greatest fishing grounds, including the Grand Banks and Georges Bank of eastern North America, are now essentially closed following their collapse. The formerly dominant fauna have been reduced to a tiny fraction of their previous abundance and effectively rendered commercially extinct in those areas.

Recognizing that a basic shift has occurred, the members of the United Nations's Food and Agriculture Organization (a body that encouraged the expansion of large-scale industrial fishing during the 1980s) recently concluded that the operation of the world's fisheries cannot be sustained. They now acknowledge that substantial damage has already been done to the marine environment and to the many economies that depend on this crucial natural resource.

Such sobering assessments are echoed in the U.S. by the National Academy of Sciences. It reported in 1995 that human actions have caused drastic reductions in many of the preferred species of edible fish and that changes induced in composition and abundance of marine animals and plants are extensive enough to endanger the functioning of marine ecosystems. Although the scientists involved in that study noted that fishing constitutes just one of many human activities that threaten the oceans, they ranked it as the most serious.

Indeed, the environmental problems facing the seas are in some ways more pressing than those on land. Daniel Pauly of the Fisheries Center at the University of British Columbia and Villy Christensen of the International Center for Living Aquatic Resources Management in Manila have pointed out that the vast majority of shallow continental shelves have been scarred by fishing, whereas large untouched tracts of rain forest still exist. For those who work with living marine resources, the damage is not at all subtle. Vaughn C. Anthony, a scientist formerly with the National Marine Fisheries Service, has said simply: "Any dumb fool knows there's no fish around."

A War on Fishes

How did this collapse happen? An explosion of fishing technologies occurred during the 1950s and 1960s. During that time, fishers adapted various military technologies to hunting on the high seas. Radar allowed boats to navigate in total fog, and sonar made it possible to detect schools of fish deep under the oceans' opaque blanket. Electronic navigation aids such as LORAN (Long-Range Navigation) and satellite positioning systems turned the trackless sea into a grid so that vessels could return to within 15 meters of a chosen location, such as sites where fish gathered and bred. Ships can now receive satellite weather maps of water-temperature fronts, indicating where fish will be traveling. Some vessels work in concert with aircraft used to spot fish.

Many industrial fishing vessels are floating factories deploying gear of enormous proportions: 129 kilometers of submerged longlines with thousands of baited hooks, bag-shaped trawl nets large enough to engulf 12 jumbo jetliners and 64-kilometer-long drift nets (still in use by some countries). Pressure from industrial fishing is so intense that 80 to 90 percent of the fish in some populations are removed every year.

For the past two decades, the fishing industry has had increasingly to face the result of extracting fish faster than these populations could reproduce. Fishers have countered loss of preferred fish by switching to species of lesser value, usually those positioned lower in the food web—a practice that robs larger fish, marine mammals and seabirds of food. During the 1980s, five of the less desirable species made up nearly 30 percent of the world fish catch but accounted for only 6 percent of its monetary value. Now there are virtually no untapped marine fish that can be exploited economically.

With the decline of so many species, some people have turned to raising fish to make up for the shortfall. Aquaculture has doubled its output in the past decade,

Major Fishing Regions of the World: Changes in Catch

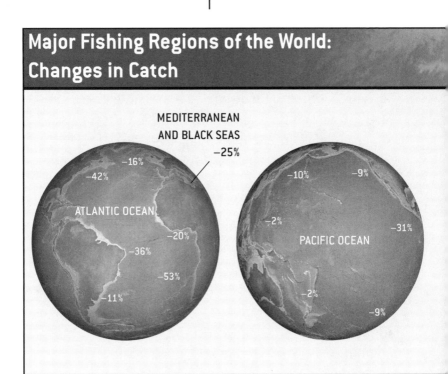

MEDITERRANEAN
AND BLACK SEAS
−25%

−16%

−42%

ATLANTIC OCEAN

−20%

−36%

−53%

−11%

−10%

−9%

−2%

PACIFIC OCEAN

−31%

−2%

−9%

increasing by about 10 million metric tons since 1985. The practice now provides more freshwater fish than wild fisheries do. Saltwater salmon farming also rivals the wild catch, and about half the shrimp now sold are raised in ponds. Overall, aquaculture supplies one third of the fish eaten by people.

Unfortunately, the development of aquaculture has not reduced the pressure on wild populations. Strangely, it may do the opposite. Shrimp farming has created a demand for otherwise worthless catch that can be used as feed. In some countries, shrimp farmers are now investing in trawl nets with fine mesh to catch

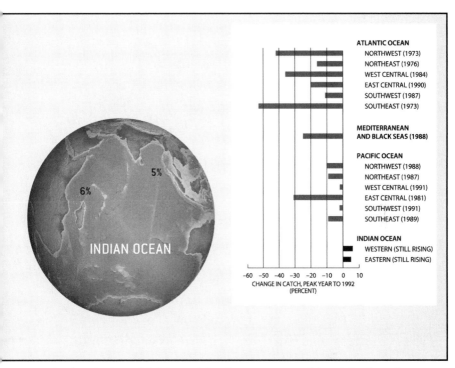

Regional takes of fish have fallen in most areas of the globe (*gray*), having reached their peak values anywhere from seven to 25 years ago. (The year of the peak catch is shown in parentheses.) Only in the Indian Ocean region, where modern methods of mechanized fishing are just now taking hold, have marine catches been on the increase. (Black indicates average annual growth between 1988 and 1992.)

everything they can for shrimp food, a practice known as biomass fishing. Many of the catch are juveniles of valuable species, and so these fish never have the opportunity to reproduce.

Fish farms can hurt wild populations because the construction of pens along the coast often requires cutting down mangroves; the submerged roots of these salt-tolerant trees provide a natural nursery for shrimp and fish. Peter Weber of the Worldwatch Institute reports that aquaculture is one of the major reasons that half the world's mangroves have been destroyed. Aquaculture also threatens marine fish because some of its most valuable products, such as groupers, milkfish and eels, cannot be bred in captivity and are raised from newly hatched fish caught in the wild. The constant loss of young fry then leads these species even further into decline.

Aquaculture also proves a poor replacement for fishing because it requires substantial investment, land ownership and large amounts of clean water. Most of the people living on the crowded coasts of the world lack all these resources. Aquaculture as carried out in many undeveloped nations often produces only shrimp and expensive types of fish for export to richer countries, leaving most of the locals to struggle for their own needs with the oceans' declining resources.

Madhouse Economics

If the situation is so dire, why are fish so available and, in most developed nations, affordable? Seafood prices have, in fact, risen faster than those for chicken, pork or beef, and the lower cost of these foods tends to constrain the price of fish—people would turn to other meats if the expense of seafood far surpassed them.

Further price increases will also be slowed by imports, by overfishing to keep supplies high (until they crash) and by aquaculture. For instance, the construction of shrimp farms that followed the decline of many wild populations has kept prices in check.

So to some extent, the economic law of supply and demand controls the cost of fish. But no law says fisheries need to be profitable. To catch $70 billion worth of fish, the fishing industry recently incurred costs totaling $124 billion annually. Subsidies fill much of the $54 billion in deficits. These artificial supports include fuel-tax exemptions, price controls, low-interest loans and outright grants for gear or infrastructure. Such massive subsidies arise from the efforts of many governments to preserve employment despite the self-destruction of so many fisheries.

These incentives have for many years enticed investors to finance more fishing ships than the seas' resources could possibly support. Between 1970 and 1990, the world's industrial fishing fleet grew at twice the rate of the global catch, fully doubling in the total tonnage of vessels and in number. This armada finally achieved twice the capacity needed to extract what the oceans could sustainably produce. Economists and managers refer to this situation as overcapitalization. Curiously, fishers would have been able to catch as much with no new vessels at all. One U.S. study found that the annual profits of the yellowtail flounder fishery could increase from zero to $6 million by removing more than 100 boats.

Because this excessive capacity rapidly depletes the amount of fish available, profitability often plummets, reducing the value of ships on the market. Unable to sell their chief asset without major financial loss, owners of these vessels are forced to keep fishing to repay their loans and are caught in an economic trap. They often exercise substantial political pressure so that government regulators will not reduce allowable takes. This common pattern has become widely recognized. Even the U.N. now acknowledges that by enticing too many participants, high levels of subsidy ultimately generate severe economic and environmental hardship.

A World Growing Hungrier

While the catch of wild marine fish declines, the number of people in the world increases every year by about 100 million, an amount equal to the current population of Mexico. Maintaining the present rate of consumption in the face of such growth will require that by 2010 approximately 19 million additional metric tons of seafood become available every year. To achieve this level, aquaculture would have to double in the next 15 years, and wild fish populations would have to be restored to allow higher sustainable catches.

Technical innovations may also help produce human food from species currently used to feed livestock. But even if all the fish that now go to these animals—a third of the world catch—were eaten by people, today's average consumption could hold for only about 20 years. Beyond that time, even improved conservation of wild fish would not be able to keep pace with human population growth. The next century will therefore witness the heretofore unthinkable exhaustion of the oceans' natural ability to satisfy humanity's demand for food from the seas.

To manage this limited resource in the best way possible will clearly require a solid understanding of marine biology and ecology. But substantial difficulties will undoubtedly arise in fashioning scientific information into intelligent policies and in translating these regulations into practice. Managers of fisheries as well as policymakers have for the most part ignored the numerous national and international stock assessments done in past years.

Where regulators have set limits, some fishers have not adhered to them. From 1986 to 1992, distant water fleets fishing on the international part of the Grand Banks off the coast of Canada removed 16 times the quotas for cod, flounder and redfish set by the Northwest Atlantic Fisheries Organization. When Canadian officials seized a Spanish fishing boat near the Grand Banks in 1995, they found two sets of logbooks—one recording true operations and one faked for the authorities. They also discovered nets with illegally small mesh and 350 metric tons of juvenile Greenland halibut. None of the fish on board were mature enough to have reproduced. Such selfish disregard for regulations helped to destroy the Grand Banks fishery.

Although the U.N. reports that about 70 percent of the world's edible fish, crustaceans and mollusks are in urgent need of managed conservation, no country can be viewed as generally successful in fisheries

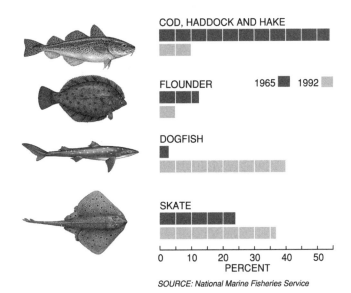

COD, HADDOCK AND HAKE

FLOUNDER   1965 ■   1992 □

DOGFISH

SKATE

0   10   20   30   40   50
PERCENT

SOURCE: *National Marine Fisheries Service*

Relative abundance of common fishes in the Gulf of Maine has changed drastically because of overfishing. The horizontal bars indicate the fraction of the catch made up of each of these species in 1965 as compared with 1992.

management. International cooperation has been even harder to come by. If a country objects to the restrictions of a particular agreement, it just ignores them.

In 1991, for instance, several countries arranged to reduce their catches of swordfish from the Atlantic; Spain and the U.S. complied with the limitations (set at 15 percent less than 1988 levels), but Japan's catch rose 70 percent, Portugal's landings increased by 120 percent and Canada's take nearly tripled. Norway has decided unilaterally to resume hunting minke whales despite an international moratorium. Japan's hunting

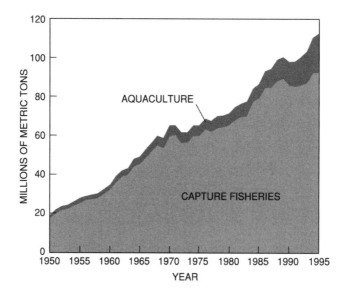

Fish supplies derived from aquaculture continue to rise steadily, but the total amount available from capture fisheries (which provide the greatest share of the global yield) has entered a period of minimal growth over the past decade.

of minke whales, ostensibly for scientific purposes, supplies meat that is sold for food and maintains a market that supports illegal whaling around the globe.

Innocent Bystanders

In virtually every kind of fishery, people inadvertently capture forms of marine life that collectively are known as bycatch or bykill. In the world's commercial fisheries, one of every four animals taken from the sea is unwanted. Fishers simply discard the remains of these numerous creatures overboard.

Bycatch involves a variety of marine life, such as species without commercial value and young fish too small to sell. In 1990 high-seas drift nets tangled 42 million animals that were not targeted, including diving seabirds and marine mammals. Such massive losses prompted the U.N. to enact a global ban on large-scale drift nets (those longer than 2.5 kilometers)—although Italy, France and Ireland, among other countries, continue to deploy them.

In some coastal areas, fishing nets set near the sea bottom routinely ensnare small dolphins. Losses to fisheries of several marine mammals—the baiji of eastern Asia, the Mexican vaquita (the smallest type of dolphin known), Hector's dolphins in the New Zealand region and the Mediterranean monk seal— put those species' survival at risk.

Seabirds are also killed when they try to eat the bait attached to fishing lines as these are played out from ships. Rosemary Gales, a research scientist at the Parks and Wildlife Service in Hobart, Tasmania, estimates that in the Southern Hemisphere more than 40,000 albatross are hooked and drowned every year after grabbing at squid used as bait on longlines being set for bluefin tuna. This level of mortality endangers six of the 14 species of these majestic wandering seabirds.

In some fisheries, bykill exceeds target catch. In 1992 in the Bering Sea, fishers discarded 16 million red king crabs, keeping only about three million. Trawling for shrimp produces more bykill than any other type of fishing and accounts for more than a third of the global total. Discarded creatures outnumber shrimp taken by anywhere from 125 to 830 percent. In the Gulf of Mexico shrimp fishery, 12 million juvenile snappers and 2,800 metric tons of sharks are discarded annually. Worldwide, fishers dispose of about six million sharks every year—half of those caught. And these statistics probably underestimate the magnitude of the waste: much bycatch goes unreported.

There remain, however, some glimmers of hope. The bykill of sea turtles in shrimp trawls had been a

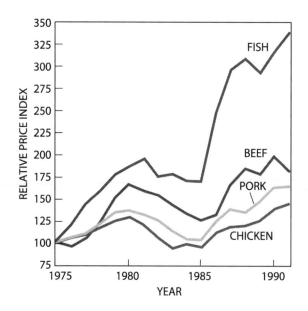

Export prices for fish have exceeded those for beef, chicken and pork by a substantial margin over the past two decades. To facilitate comparison, the price of each meat is scaled to 100 for 1975.

constant plague on these creatures in U.S. waters (the National Research Council estimated that up to 55,000 adult turtles die this way every year). But these deaths are being reduced by recently mandated "excluder devices" that shunt the animals out a trap door in the nets.

Perhaps the best-publicized example of bycatch involved up to 400,000 dolphins killed annually by fishers netting Pacific yellowfin tuna. Over three decades since the tuna industry began using huge nets, the eastern spinner dolphin population fell 80 percent, and the numbers of offshore spotted dolphin plummeted by more than 50 percent. These declines led to the use of so-called dolphin-safe methods (begun in 1990) whereby fishers shifted from netting around dolphin schools to netting around logs and other floating objects.

This approach has been highly successful: dolphin kills went down to 4,000 in 1993. Unfortunately, dolphin-safe netting methods are not safe for immature tuna, billfish, turtle or shark. On average, for every 1,000 nets set around dolphin herds, fishers inadvertently capture 500 dolphins, 52 billfish, 10 sea turtles and no sharks. In contrast, typical bycatch from the same number of sets around floating objects includes only two dolphins but also 654 billfish, 102 sea turtles and 13,958 sharks. In addition, many juvenile tuna are caught under floating objects.

One solution to the bycatch from nets would be to fish for tuna with poles and lines, as was practiced commercially in the 1950s. That switch would entail hiring back bigger crews, such as those laid off when the tuna fishery first mechanized its operations.

The recent reductions in the bycatch of dolphins and turtles provide a reminder that although the state of the world's fisheries is precarious, there are also reasons for optimism. Scientific grasp of the problems is still developing, yet sufficient knowledge has been amassed to understand how the difficulties can be rectified. Clearly, one of the most important steps that could be taken to prevent overfishing and excessive bycatch is to remove the subsidies for fisheries that would otherwise be financially incapable of existing off the oceans' wildlife—but are now quite capable of depleting it.

Where fishes have been protected, they have rebounded, along with the social and economic activities they support. The resurgence of striped bass along the eastern coast of the U.S. is probably the best example in the world of a species that was allowed to recoup through tough management and an intelligent rebuilding plan.

Recent progress provides added hope. The 1995 U.N. agreement on high-seas fishing and the 1996 Sustainable Fisheries Act in the U.S., along with regional and local marine conservation efforts, could— if faithfully implemented—help to guide the world toward a sane and vital future for life in the oceans.

The Author

Carl Safina earned his doctorate in ecology in 1987 at Rutgers University, where he studied natural dynamics among seabirds, prey fishes and predatory fishes. He founded and now directs the National Audubon Society's Living Oceans Program. He also teaches at Yale University, serves as deputy chair of the World Conservation Union's Shark Specialist Group, is a founding member of the Marine Fish Conservation Network and was formerly on the Mid-Atlantic Fisheries Management Council. Safina received the Pew Charitable Trust's Scholars Award in Conservation and the Environment. He has fished commercially and for sport.

During the past fifty years, many species of frogs, toads, salamanders, and newts have mysteriously declined in number. A study in 2004 found that at least 122 species have become extinct since 1980. Of the existing 5,743 species, 32 percent are endangered and may become extinct in the not too distant future. If you are not an animal lover, you may wonder why we should care about amphibians, or any other animal for that matter. The answer is that our fate is linked to theirs.

As this next article reveals, ultraviolet light rays have been damaging DNA in amphibian eggs and reducing survival rates. Since this did not always happen, the finding suggests that more harmful rays of sunlight are reaching

*Earth's surface. This, in turn, indicates that holes
exist in the upper atmosphere's ozone layer. By
repairing the holes in the ozone, we may save
the lives of amphibians and possibly our own
lives, since overexposure to ultraviolet light can
result in certain forms of cancer, especially skin
cancer. —JV*

"The Puzzle of Declining Amphibian Populations"
by Andrew R. Blaustein and David B. Wake
Scientific American, **April 1995**

Perhaps our fascination with frogs and other amphibians
starts in childhood, with the discovery of tadpoles and
the observation of their metamorphosis. But for many
adults today, interest stems more from observation of
another type of change: amphibian populations in
many parts of the world seem to be dwindling, and
some groups are disappearing from their native habitats
completely. The loss—first recognized as a global
phenomenon in 1990—deserves attention not only
because it is disturbing in its own right but also because
frogs and their kin (mainly toads and salamanders)
may serve as indicators of the overall condition of the
environment.

Amphibians are valuable as gauges of the planet's
health for a few reasons. First, they are in intimate
contact with many components of their natural
surroundings. For example, as larvae, frogs live in water,

but as adults most find themselves at least partially on land. Their moist, delicate skins are thin enough to allow respiration, and their unshelled eggs are directly exposed to soil, water and sunlight. As larvae, they are herbivores and as adults, carnivores. Because amphibians sample many parts of the environment, their health reflects the combined effects of many separate influences in their ecosystem. Second, these animals are good monitors of local conditions because they are homebodies, remaining in fairly confined regions for their entire lives. What happens to frogs and their brethren is happening where humans live and might affect our species as well.

Finally, amphibians are so varied that any single characteristic, unique to the class, can be dismissed as the cause of the dwindling numbers; hence, we suspect that environmental factors are indeed the main cause for their decline. Amphibians are diverse in color, form, behavior and natural history. They vary in physical size, reproductive capacity and population density. And they are found in many ecosystems and habitats, including deserts, grasslands and forests, from sea level to high mountaintops. Although these creatures are most abundant in the tropics, they are also common in temperate zones and can even be found at higher latitudes, such as in Alaska and northern Canada.

Which environmental factors might account for the rapid decline of animals that have managed, over hundreds of millions of years, to survive events that led to the mass extinction of many species, including the dinosaurs? The explanations that have been proposed are almost as diverse as the amphibian species in jeopardy, ranging from destruction of habitat to natural fluctuations in population size.

One or more of the suggestions do seem to explain the shrinkage of many populations. But in other cases, the reasons for the declines are not obvious. In those instances, the damage may be caused by subtle, interacting aspects of regional or even global conditions. In particular, recent work, completed last spring, has led to the surprising discovery that stratospheric ozone depletion may well be harming amphibian species in some parts of the world.

We began to suspect that the ozone problem might play a role as a result of studies that one of us (Blaustein) and his students began in Oregon in 1979. The most recent experiments, often conducted at relatively high elevations (above 4,000 feet) in remote, undisturbed parts of the Cascade Mountains, examined various aspects of life for several species of amphibians monitored from the egg, or embryonic, stage through the tadpole phase and into adulthood. Although the group intended to carry out a straightforward survey of amphibian behavior and ecology, it discovered some unexpected results.

The Role of Ultraviolet Rays

As part of the research, the team documented massive die-offs of fertilized eggs in two species in particular: the Cascades frog (*Rana cascadae*) and the western toad (*Bufo boreas*). Additionally, over the course of 10 years, the group noticed that the numbers of adults of these species were dropping. The investigators guessed that the shrinking numbers of adult frogs and toads could result from the fact that so few fertilized eggs survived, and thus they began to explore the reasons for the damage to the eggs.

The researchers quickly ruled out the possibility that the chemistry of the water where the animals were laying their eggs was at fault. They brought eggs into the laboratory and reared the resulting embryos in a sample of the same lake water in which other eggs left behind had perished. The embryonic frogs and toads developed and hatched normally in the laboratory. Furthermore, chemical analyses of the lakes and ponds where eggs died revealed no obvious pollution or excess acidity.

By the late 1980s another possible cause of egg destruction had presented itself. Scientists in several disciplines documented a decrease in the stratospheric ozone shield that blocks most ultraviolet rays from reaching the ground. These observations led Blaustein and his co-workers to wonder whether increased exposure to ultraviolet radiation could explain the reproductive problems they had seen. They also thought it might explain why many of the amphibian species known to be in decline were mountain dwellers that lay their eggs in open, often shallow, water. Such eggs undergo prolonged exposure to sunlight and thus to any ultraviolet radiation that passes through the ozone shield.

The researchers speculated that excessive exposure to ultraviolet radiation could be contributing to the problems of the Cascades frog and western toad because they were aware of evidence showing that ultraviolet rays can damage plant and animal life. In particular, ultraviolet-B radiation (with a wavelength ranging from 280 to 320 nanometers), in the middle of the ultraviolet spectrum, is especially harmful to living organisms. In humans, for example, it can suppress the immune system, cause cataracts and contribute to skin cancer. What is more, as early as the mid-1970s, Robert C. Worrest of Oregon State University had shown that ultraviolet-B rays could cause amphibian embryos to develop abnormally in the laboratory.

Few experiments, however, had considered the consequences of ultraviolet radiation on amphibians or other animals in nature. Blaustein and his colleagues therefore set out to determine whether increasing levels of ultraviolet-B radiation could play a role in the decline of amphibian populations in the wild. The team for this enterprise included ecologist Susan C. Walls and molecular geneticists John B. Hays and Peter D. Hoffman, as well as graduate students D. Grant Hokit and Joseph M. Kiesecker, all then at Oregon State University.

The crew based its procedure on an understanding of how ultraviolet radiation affects DNA. When DNA absorbs energy from such rays, the bonds that hold the molecule together break, and new structures are formed. The changes in DNA can disrupt the functioning of cells and may even kill them. But many organisms have the capacity to repair DNA damage caused by ultraviolet radiation. As part of this process, some of those organisms—including certain species of algae, plants, fish, marsupials and amphibians—activate an enzyme known as photolyase, which removes the harmful structures.

By measuring the amount of photolyase produced in the eggs of various amphibians, the workers found that levels varied among species. Most important, they determined that species with falling populations were generally those with eggs that produced low levels of photolyase—and therefore had little protection from ultraviolet radiation.

The species with the most photolyase, the Pacific treefrog (*Hyla regilla*), was not suffering from a decrease in population. Pacific treefrog eggs have about three times as much photolyase as do Cascades frog eggs and six times as much as western toad eggs. Hence, it seems that because the embryonic Cascades frogs and western toads produce low levels of photolyase, they do not make enough of the enzyme to counteract exposure to unusually high amounts of ultraviolet radiation. This lack of protection in turn may lead to the high mortality observed for the eggs and explain why these two species are candidates for threatened status in some states.

Once the group noticed a correlation between lack of protection from ultraviolet radiation and declining population, the next challenge was to find supporting evidence that the rays were actually at fault. The team collected freshly laid eggs of Cascades frogs, western toads, Pacific treefrogs and northwestern salamanders (*Ambystoma gracile*). The salamanders, like the other three groups, lay their fertilized eggs in open, shallow water. Additionally, these salamanders produce extremely low levels of photolyase.

Exposed Eggs Fail to Hatch

The researchers placed the eggs in the bottom of screened enclosures. Atop one third of the containers they placed a cover of clear plastic (Mylar) that shielded the eggs from ultraviolet-B radiation. A second set remained open, fully exposing the eggs. On the remaining third of the boxes, they placed a clear cover of plastic acetate that allowed transmission of radiation. This treatment served as a control to ensure that the outcome observed in shaded boxes was not caused by the covers.

The workers placed a total of 48 boxes randomly around lakes and ponds at several different sites where each species normally lays its eggs. The experiments on frog and toad eggs were conducted in the spring of 1993 at relatively high altitudes (greater than 4,000 feet) in the Cascade Range of Oregon. The team studied the eggs of the northwestern salamanders in the foothills of the Oregon Coast Range (600-foot elevation) during 1994. The research continued until all the eggs either hatched or perished, a process that took from one to two weeks because of varying weather conditions.

If it were true that an inability to combat the harm caused by excessive exposure to ultraviolet radiation was destroying the eggs of many amphibian species, the producers of the lower amounts of photolyase would be expected to fare worse, and the producers of higher levels, better. The results of the field experiments were dramatic. More than 90 percent of the northwestern salamander eggs exposed to ultraviolet-B radiation died (compared with 45 percent of eggs protected from the rays). More than 40 percent of the exposed western toad and Cascades frog eggs died (compared with 10 to 20 percent of the shielded eggs). In contrast, almost all the eggs of Pacific treefrogs in all three experimental treatments hatched successfully.

Clearly, amphibian eggs in wild populations were dying from exposure to ultraviolet-B radiation. And this damage to the eggs was very possibly contributing to the decline in adult populations that had been observed earlier. Investigators do not know whether northwestern salamanders are disappearing, but if these experiments are any indication, chances are good that those creatures, too, are in jeopardy.

By what mechanism does ultraviolet radiation lead to the destruction of amphibian eggs and embryos? Other research by Blaustein and his colleagues may have uncovered a partial explanation. It turns out that since the late 1980s, increasing numbers of amphibians in Oregon have been sickened by the fungus *Saprolegnia*, which is found naturally in lakes and ponds. The fungus is also known to infect hatchery-reared fishes, especially salmon and trout. Perhaps fish that have been released into lakes and are infected with *Saprolegnia* contaminate amphibian eggs in those waters. Because ultraviolet rays can impair immune function in many animals, it seems reasonable to guess that some amount of egg damage in amphibians is caused by an ultraviolet-induced breakdown in the ability of amphibian embryos to resist infection by the fungus.

Aside from harming fertilized eggs, ultraviolet radiation may contribute to declines in amphibian populations by reducing the supply of aquatic insects on which frogs and their relatives feed. High levels of such radiation have been known to kill insect larvae as well as aquatic algae.

The work in Oregon has provided one potentially important clue to the mystery of amphibian disappearance. But many questions still remain. How many eggs can fail to hatch before a population itself begins to decline? Does ultraviolet radiation harm growing tadpoles that congregate in shallow water? And are adults that bask in sunlight affected directly by ultraviolet radiation? The two of us are now beginning to focus on these issues.

The Threat of Habitat Destruction

As worrisome as the increase in ultraviolet radiation seems to be, it is not the only potentially significant cause of shrinkage of amphibian populations. In the Monteverde cloud forest of Costa Rica and in the

Australian rain forests, for example, amphibians typically live under a dense foliage canopy and hide their eggs. Yet many of their numbers are also in decline.

One of us (Wake) has been investigating causes of dwindling amphibian populations since the 1970s, when the first hints of a problem began to emerge. The issue is indeed compelling, for although evidence of falling numbers is strong in various parts of the world, in other areas amphibians appear to be doing well. This puzzling situation has prompted us and others to examine closely the possible reasons for the declines we have seen.

No single explanation fits every case, but all seem to be important to one degree or another. Destruction and modification of habitat are probably the most serious causes of falling amphibian populations. Like other animals, amphibians are threatened when forests are destroyed and wetlands are filled in or paved. Indeed, such activities probably account for the decrease in a majority of species threatened today.

In one striking example of this phenomenon, a recent survey in western North Carolina showed that clear-cutting of national forests leads to the deaths of enormous numbers of salamanders every year. Although most of the species involved have relatively large geographic ranges and are not in danger of extinction, the findings have distressing implications for amphibians living in tropical America, Africa and Asia. There many amphibians are more vulnerable because they have very limited geographic ranges.

Pollution Plays a Part

Pollutants, too, may have altered amphibian populations in some parts of the world, although data on the effects of pollution on these creatures are sparse. Some evidence suggests that acid rain and snow, fungicides, herbicides, insecticides and industrial chemicals may all act by impairing the reproduction and development of amphibians. Certain synthetic compounds can mimic the activity of naturally occurring hormones. Examination of birds, fish and reptiles indicates that these substances can have drastic consequences, such as a reduction in sperm count and the alteration of male genitalia.

Diseases—possibly related to environmental pollution—seem to jeopardize some amphibians as well. Recall, for instance, that eggs of the Cascades frog and western toad are vulnerable to the fungus *Saprolegnia* and that susceptibility to the fungal infection is probably increased by exposure to excessive ultraviolet radiation. Further, the late Arthur N. Bragg, when he was at the University of Oklahoma, showed that *Saprolegnia* can destroy whole populations of tadpoles, although this discovery has been largely overlooked as a cause of amphibian deaths.

So far only a few studies have linked a disease to the extinction of an entire population of amphibians. Investigators have found, however, that the bacterium *Aeromonas hydrophila* may have triggered the disappearance of several populations of western toads in Colorado.

The bacterium is highly contagious and has been implicated as well in the death of adult frogs, toads and salamanders in several other states.

Some scientists attribute the apparent shrinkage of amphibian populations to natural fluctuations in population size. Yet certain long-term investigations show a more or less steady decline in the number of amphibians over the past 20 to 30 years—an indication that in some populations other forces are at work.

Additional causes may explain isolated cases of dropping numbers of amphibians. Some populations may be decreasing because they are collected for human consumption. In France, for instance, the demand for frog legs is tremendous: the French eat 3,000 to 4,000 metric tons of them a year. Some 20,000 frogs must be sacrificed in order to supply a single metric ton of legs. And before the turn of the century, red-legged frogs (*R. aurora*) were probably overharvested as a food source in Oregon and California.

Ironically, efforts to boost amphibian populations in the western U.S. probably created more problems for the native amphibians there and provided an illustration of yet another possible cause of population declines: the introduction of nonnative species to an area.

To make up for decreases in the number of red-legged frogs, inhabitants of Oregon and California introduced the bullfrog (*R. catesbeiana*). This animal, with its voracious appetite, competed with or preyed on native amphibians in its new habitat. Noting that the introduced bullfrogs have become quite abundant in some places where the original frog species have declined, many biologists have recently suggested that bullfrogs are a major cause of falling numbers. And at least two ongoing studies have directly linked the introduction of bullfrogs to the dwindling of native frog species.

Similarly, introduction of fish into an ecosystem may hurt amphibians, especially in regions with few species of fish, low numbers of individual fish or no fish at all. In the southern Sierra Nevada Mountains of California, the introduction of salmon and trout into streams has been implicated in the demise of mountain yellow-legged frogs (R. muscosa). These fish species directly harm amphibians by eating eggs, tadpoles and even adults, but they also have a broader and potentially more profound result.

Many separate amphibian populations are linked to one another by streams patrolled by few or no fish. These links are important because frogs and their relatives are extremely vulnerable to changes in their local habitat, and they rely on the appearance of occasional migrants to help them rebuild diminished communities. The addition of new fish species into an area can block migration between communities and thus prevent the reconstitution of endangered populations.

Dangerous Consequences

The disappearance of amphibians represents more than just a loss of esthetically and behaviorally appealing creatures. These animals are crucial components of many ecological communities, and they can directly benefit humans. In some ecosystems, amphibians are the most abundant vertebrates, and so their absence can seriously disrupt the functioning of the rest of the ecological community. Adult amphibians are hunters of various animals, including mosquitoes, flies, fish, birds and even small mammals. Also, amphibian larvae serve as a food supply for aquatic insects, fish, mammals and birds. Destruction of frogs, toads and salamanders thus has repercussions elsewhere in the food chain.

From the perspective of humans, amphibians represent a storehouse of pharmaceutical products waiting to be tapped fully. Hundreds of chemical secretions have been isolated from amphibian skin, and scientists are just beginning to learn how valuable these substances may be. Some of these compounds are already used as painkillers and in treatment of victims of traumas ranging from burns to heart attacks. Others are being investigated for their antibacterial and antiviral properties. As amphibians disappear, potential cures for a number of maladies go with them.

The evidence that depletion of the ozone shield in the stratosphere can harm the developing embryos of amphibians highlights the complexity of the forces leading to the elimination of species. Nevertheless, habitat degradation and destruction clearly remain the most powerful causes of amphibian disappearance around the world. If habitat modification occurs slowly enough—as it did for 3,000 years in western

Europe—amphibians can adjust and even adapt to human-induced alterations. But many of the changes we have discussed, such as rises in ultraviolet levels and in the amounts of pollutants in the environment, have occurred so rapidly that species with long generation times often cannot adapt quickly enough.

There are a lot more species of amphibians than scientists studying them. Of those that are known, many have been seen only once, at the time of their discovery. The number of species described continues to increase at a rate of 1 to 2 percent a year. If, as we believe, many of these species are at risk, a wonderfully diverse group of creatures is vanishing from the planet at a time when study of them has just begun.

The Authors

Andrew R. Blaustein and David B. Wake combine their interests in behavioral ecology and evolutionary biology in their studies of amphibians. Blaustein, an ecologist, is a professor at Oregon State University. Wake, an evolutionary biologist, is a professor at the University of California, Berkeley. Both Blaustein and Wake belong to the Species Survival Commission of the World Conservation Union. Blaustein is co-chairman of the Pacific Northwest Section of the Task Force on Declining Amphibian Populations. Wake was the founding chairman of the International Task Force on Declining Amphibian Populations.

The prior articles have discussed particular species that are imperiled, but something much more ominous may be happening even as you read this book. According to many researchers, up to half of the world's species could become extinct within the next fifty years. Such a mass extinction has not occurred since the end of the Cretaceous period, when the dinosaurs perished. The situation is dire. As scientist David S. Woodruff indicates in the following article, "Many of the species in trouble today are in fact already members of the doomed, living dead."

Earth already has withstood at least five major extinctions. Unlike past extinctions, humans likely are to blame for the current wave of death. Scientists are concerned that particular species and ecosystems are not the only things at stake. The integrity of underlying evolutionary processes that shape us and the planet may also be at risk.

Despite the gloomy predictions, all hope is not lost. A solution that has yielded some success is for conservation groups to speak not with words, but with money. Groups such as the Nature Conservancy have been bidding against logging companies and other commercial groups for control of wilderness areas. The U.S. government and leaders of other nations often have demonstrated little concern for environmental issues, so individuals and organizations have had to take the matter into their own hands. —JV

"On the Termination of Species"
by W. Wayt Gibbs
Scientific American, November 2001

HILO, HAWAII—Among the scientists gathered here in August at the annual meeting of the Society for Conservation Biology, the despair was almost palpable. "I'm just glad I'm retiring soon and won't be around to see everything disappear," said P. Dee Boersma, former president of the society, during the opening night's dinner. Other veteran field biologists around the table murmured in sullen agreement.

At the next morning's keynote address, Robert M. May, a University of Oxford zoologist who presides over the Royal Society and until last year served as chief scientific adviser to the British government, did his best to disabuse any remaining optimists of their rosy outlook. According to his latest rough estimate, the extinction rate—the pace at which species vanish—accelerated during the past 100 years to roughly 1,000 times what it was before humans showed up. Various lines of argument, he explained, "suggest a speeding up by a further factor of 10 over the next century or so . . . And that puts us squarely on the breaking edge of the sixth great wave of extinction in the history of life on Earth."

From there, May's lecture grew more depressing. Biologists and conservationists alike, he complained, are afflicted with a "total vertebrate chauvinism." Their bias toward mammals, birds and fish—when

Overview/*Extinction Rates*

- Eminent ecologists warn that humans are causing a mass extinction event of a severity not seen since the age of dinosaurs came to an end 65 million years ago. But paleontologists and statisticians have called such comparisons into doubt.
- It is hard to know how fast species are disappearing. Models based on the speed of tropical deforestation or on the growth of endangered species lists predict rising extinction rates. But biologists' bias towards plants and vertebrates, which represent a minority of life, undermine these predictions. Because 90 percent of species do not yet have names, let alone censuses, they are impossible to verify.
- In the face of uncertainty about the decline of biodiversity and its economic value, scientists are debating whether rare species should be the focus of conservation. Perhaps, some suggest, we should first try to save relatively pristine— and inexpensive—land where evolution can progress unaffected by human activity.

most of the diversity of life lies elsewhere—undermines scientists' ability to predict reliably the scope and consequences of biodiversity loss. It also raises troubling questions about the high-priority "hotspots" that environmental groups are scrambling to identify and preserve.

"Ultimately we have to ask ourselves why we care" about the planet's portfolio of species and its diminishment, May said. "This central question is a political and social question of values, one in which the voice of conservation scientists has no particular standing." Unfortunately, he concluded, of "the three kinds of argument we use to try to persuade politicians that all this is important . . . none is totally compelling."

Although May paints a truly dreadful picture, his is a common view for a field in which best-sellers carry titles such as *Requiem for Nature*. But is despair justified? *The Skeptical Environmentalist*, the new English translation of a recent book by Danish statistician Bjørn Lomborg, charges that reports of the death of biodiversity have been greatly exaggerated. In the face of such external skepticism, internal uncertainty and public apathy, some scientists are questioning the conservation movement's overriding emphasis on preserving rare species and the threatened hotspots in which they are concentrated. Perhaps, they suggest, we should focus instead on saving something equally at risk but even more valuable: evolution itself.

Doom . . .

May's claim that humans appear to be causing a cataclysm of extinctions more severe than any since the one that erased the dinosaurs 65 million years ago may shock those who haven't followed the biodiversity issue. But it prompted no gasps from the conservation biologists. They have heard variations of this dire forecast since at least 1979, when Norman Myers guessed in *The Sinking Ark* that 40,000 species lose their last member each year and that one million would be extinct by 2000. In the 1980s Thomas Lovejoy similarly predicted that 15 to 20 percent would die off by 2000; Paul Ehrlich figured half would be gone by now. "I'm reasonably certain that [the elimination of one fifth of species] didn't happen," says Kirk O. Winemiller, a fish biologist at Texas A&M University who just finished a review of the scientific literature on extinction rates.

More recent projections factor in a slightly slower demise because some doomed species have hung on longer than anticipated. Indeed, a few have even returned from the grave, "It was discovered only this summer that the Bavarian vole, continental Eurasia's one and only presumed extinct mammal [since 1500], is in fact still with us," says Ross D. E. MacPhee, curator of mammalogy at the American Museum of Natural History (AMNH) in New York City.

Still, in the 1999 edition of his often-quoted book *The Diversity of Life*, Harvard University biologist E. O. Wilson cites current estimates that between 1 and 10 percent of species are extinguished every decade, at least 27,000 a year. Michael J. Novacek, AMNH's provost of science, wrote in a review article this spring that "figures approaching 30 percent extermination of all species by the mid-21st century are not unrealistic."

And in a 1998 survey of biologists, 70 percent said they believed that a mass extinction is in progress; a third of them expected to lose 20 to 50 percent of the world's species within 30 years.

"Although these assertions of massive extinctions of species have been repeated everywhere you look, they do not equate with the available evidence," Lomborg argues in *The Skeptical Environmentalist.* A professor of statistics and political science at the University of Århus, he alleges that environmentalists have ignored recent evidence that tropical deforestation is not taking the toll that was feared. "No well-investigated group of animals shows a pattern of loss that is consistent with greatly heightened extinction rates," MacPhee concurs. The best models, Lomborg suggests, project an extinction rate of 0.15 percent of species per decade, "not a catastrophe but a problem—one of many that mankind still needs to solve."

. . . or Gloom?

"It's a tough question to put numbers on," Wilson allows. May agrees but says "that isn't an argument for not asking the question" of whether a mass extinction event is upon us.

To answer that question, we need to know three things: the natural (or "background") extinction rate, the current rate and whether the pace of extinction is steady or changing. The first step, Wilson explains, is to work out the mean life span of a species from the fossil record. "The background extinction rate is then

The Portfolio of Life

How severe is the extinction crisis? That depends in large part on how many species there are altogether. The greater the number, the more species will die out every year from natural causes and the more new ones will naturally appear. But although the general outlines of the tree of life are clear, scientists are unsure how many twigs lie at the end of each branch. When it comes to bacteria, viruses, protists, and archaea (a whole kingdom of single-celled life-forms discovered just a few decades ago), microbiologists have only vague notions of how many branches there are.

Birds, fish, mammals and plants are the exceptions. Sizing up the global workforce of about 5,000 professional taxonomists, zoologist Robert M. May of the University of Oxford noted that about equal numbers study vertebrates, plants and invertebrates. "You may wish to think this record reflects some judicious appreciation of what's important," he says. "My view of that is: absolute garbage. Whether you are interested in how ecosystems evolved, their current functioning or how they are likely to respond to climate change, you're going to learn a lot more by looking at soil microorganisms than at charismatic vertebrates."

For every group except birds, says Peter Hammond of the National History Museum in London, new species are now being discovered faster than ever before, thanks to several new international projects. An All Taxa Biodiversity

Inventory under way in Great Smoky Mountains National Park in North Carolina and Tennessee has discovered 115 species—80 percent of them insects or arachnids—in its first 18 months of work. Last year 40 scientists formed the All Species Project, a society devoted to the (probably quixotic) goal of cataloguing every living species, microbes included, within 25 years.

Other projects, such as the Global Biodiversity Information Facility and Species2000, are building Internet databases that will codify species records that are now scattered among the world's museums and universities. If biodiversity is defined in strictly pragmatic terms as the variety of life-forms we know about, it is growing prodigiously.

the inverse of that. If species are born at random and all live exactly one million years—and it varies, but it's on that order—then that means one species in a million naturally goes extinct each year," he says.

In a 1995 article that is still cited in almost every scientific paper on this subject (even in Lomborg's book), May used a similar method to compute the background rate. He relied on estimates that put the mean species life span at five million to 10 million years, however; he thus came up with a rate that is five to 10 times lower than Wilson's. But according to paleontologist David M. Raup (then at the University of Chicago), who published some of the figures May and Wilson relied on, their calculations are seriously flawed by three false assumptions.

One is that species of plants, mammals, insects, marine invertebrates and other groups all exist for about the same time. In fact, the typical survival time appears to vary among groups by a factor of 10 or more, with mammal species among the least durable. Second, they assume that all organisms have an equal chance of making it into the fossil record. But paleontologists estimate that fewer than 4 percent of all species that ever lived are preserved as fossils. "And the species we do see are the widespread, very successful ones," Raup says. "The weak species confined to some hilltop or island all went extinct before they could be fossilized," adds John Alroy of the University of California at Santa Barbara.

The third problem is that May and Wilson use an average life span when they should use a median. Because "the vast majority of species are short-lived," Raup says, "the average is distorted by the very few that have very long life spans." All three oversimplifications underestimate the background rate—and make the current picture scarier in comparison.

Earlier this year U.C.S.B. biomathematician Helen M. Regan and several of her colleagues published the first attempt ever to correct for the strong biases, and uncertainties in the data. They looked exclusively at mammals, the best-studied group. They estimated how many of the mammals now living, and how many of those recently extinguished, would show up as fossils. They also factored in the uncertainty for each number rather than relying on best guesses. In the end they concluded that "the current rate of mammalian extinction lies between 17 and 377 times the background extinction rate." The best estimate, they wrote, is a 36- to 78-fold increase.

Regan's method is still imperfect. Comparing the past 400 years with the previous 65 million unavoidably assumes, she says, "that the current extinction rate will be sustained over millions of years." Alroy recently came up with a way to measure the speed of extinctions that doesn't suffer from such assumptions. Over the past 200 years, he figures, the rate of loss among mammal species has been some 120 times higher than natural.

A Grim Guessing Game

Attempts to figure out the current extinction rate are fraught with even more uncertainties. The international conservation organization IUCN keeps "Red Lists" of organisms suspected to be extinct in the wild. But MacPhee complains that "the IUCN methodology for recognizing extinction is not sufficiently rigorous to be reliable." He and other extinction experts have formed the Committee on Recently Extinct Organisms, which combed the Red Lists to identify those species that were clearly unique and that had not been found despite a reasonable search. They certified 60 of the 87 mammals listed by IUCN as extinct but claim that only

33 of the 92 freshwater fish presumed extinct by IUCN are definitely gone forever.

For every species falsely presumed absent, however, there may be hundreds or thousands that vanish unknown to science. "We are uncertain to a factor of 10 about how many species we share the planet with," May points out. "My guess would be roughly seven million, but credible guesses range from five to 15 million," excluding microorganisms.

Taxonomists have named approximately 1.8 million species, but biologists know almost nothing about most of them, especially the insects, nematodes and crustaceans that dominate the animal kingdom. Some 40 percent of the 400,000 known beetle species have each been recorded at just one location—and with no idea of individual species' range, scientists have no way to confirm its extinction. Even invertebrates known to be extinct often go unrecorded: when the passenger pigeon was eliminated in 1914, it took two species of parasitic lice with it. They still do not appear on IUCN's list.

"It is extremely difficult to observe an extinction; it's like seeing an airplane crash," Wilson says. Not that scientists aren't trying. Articles on the "biotic holocaust," as Myers calls it, usually figure that the vast majority of extinctions have been in the tropical Americas. Freshwater fishes are especially vulnerable, with more than a quarter listed as threatened. "I work in Venezuela, which has substantially more freshwater fishes than all of North America. After 30 years of work, we've done a reasonable job of cataloguing fish diversity there," observes Winemiller of Texas A&M, "yet we can't point to one documented case of extinction."

A similar pattern emerges for other groups of organisms, he claims. "If you are looking for hard evidence of tens or hundreds or thousands of species disappearing each year, you aren't going to find it. That could be because the database is woefully inadequate," he acknowledges. "But one shouldn't dismiss the possibility that it's not going to be the disaster everyone fears."

The Logic of Loss

The disaster scenarios are based on several independent lines of evidence that seem to point to fast and rising extinction rates. The most widely accepted is the species-area relation. "Generally speaking, as the area of habitat falls, the number of species living in it drops proportionally by the third root to the sixth root," explains Wilson, who first deduced this equation more than 30 years ago. "A middle value is the fourth root, which means that when you eliminate 90 percent of the habitat, the number of species falls by half."

"From that rough first estimate and the rate of the destruction of the tropical forest, which is about 1 percent a year," Wilson continues, "we can predict that about one quarter of 1 percent of species either become extinct immediately or are doomed to much earlier extinction." From a pool of roughly 10 million species, we should thus expect about 25,000 to evaporate annually.

Lomborg challenges that view on three grounds, however. Species-area relations were worked out by comparing the number of species on islands and do not necessarily apply to fragmented habitats on the mainland. "More than half of Costa Rica's native bird species occur in largely deforested countryside habitats, together with similar fractions of mammals and butter-flies," Stanford University biologist Gretchen Daily noted recently in *Nature*. Although they may not thrive, a large fraction of forest species may survive on farmland and in woodlots—for how long, no one yet knows.

That would help explain Lomborg's second obser-vation, which is that in both the eastern U.S. and Puerto Rico, clearance of more than 98 percent of the primary forests did not wipe out half of the bird species in them. Four centuries of logging "resulted in the extinction of only one forest bird" out of 200 in the U.S. and seven out of 60 native species in Puerto Rico, he asserts.

Such criticisms misunderstand the species-area theory, according to Stuart L. Pimm of Columbia University. "Habitat destruction acts like a cookie cutter stamping out poorly mixed dough," he wrote last year in *Nature*. "Species found only within the stamped-out area are themselves stamped out. Those found more widely are not."

Of the 200 bird types in the forests of the eastern U.S., Pimm states, all but 28 also lived elsewhere. Moreover, the forest was cleared gradually, and gradually

Extinction Filters

Survival of the fittest takes on a new meaning when humans develop a region. Among four Mediterranean climate regions, those developed more recently have lost larger fractions of their vascular plant species in modern times. Once the species least compatible with agriculture are filtered out by "artificial selection," extinction rates seem to fall.

REGION (in order of development)	EXTINCT (per 1,000)	THREATENED (percent)
Mediterranean	1.3	14.7
South African Cape	3.0	15.2
California	4.0	10.2
Western Australia	6.6	17.5

SOURCE: *"Extinctions in Mediterranean Areas."* Werner Greuter *in* Extinction Rates. *Edited by J. H. Lawton and R. H. May. Oxford University Press, 1995.*

it regrew as farmland was abandoned. So even at the low point, around 1872, woodland covered half the extent of the original forest. The species-area theory predicts that a 50 percent reduction should knock out 16 percent of the endemic species: in this case, four birds. And four species did go extinct. Lomborg discounts one of those four that may have been a subspecies and two others that perhaps succumbed to unrelated insults.

But even if the species-area equation holds, Lomborg responds, official statistics suggest that deforestation has been slowing and is now well below 1 percent a year. The U.N. Food and Agriculture Organization recently estimated that from 1990 to 2000 the world's forest cover dropped at an average annual rate of 0.2 percent (11.5 million hectares felled, minus 2.5 million hectares of new growth).

Annual forest loss was around half a percent in most of the tropics, however, and that is where the great majority of rare and threatened species live. So although "forecasters may get these figures wrong now and then, perhaps colored by a desire to sound the alarm, this is just a matter of timescale," replies Carlos A. Peres, a Brazilian ecologist at the University of East Anglia in England.

An Uncertain Future

Ecologists have tried other means to project future extinction rates. May and his co-workers watched how vertebrate species moved through the threat categories in IUCN's database over a four-year period (two years for plants), projected those very small numbers far into the future and concluded that extinction rates will rise 12- to 55-fold over the next 300 years.

Georgina M. Mace, director of science at the Zoological Society of London, came to a similar conclusion by combining models that plot survival odds for a few very well known species. Entomologist Nigel E. Stork of the Natural History Museum in London noted that a British bird is 10 times more likely than a British bug to be endangered. He then extrapolated such ratios to the rest of the world to predict 100,000 to 500,000 insect extinctions by 2300. Lomborg favors this latter model, from which he concludes that "the rate for all animals will remain below 0.208 percent per decade and probably be below 0.7 percent per 50 years."

It takes a heroic act of courage for any scientist to erect such long and broad projections on such a thin and lopsided base of data. Especially when, according to May, the data on endangered species "may tell us more about the vagaries of sampling efforts, of taxonomists' interests and of data entry than about the real changes in species' status."

Biologists have some good theoretical reasons to fear that even if mass extinction hasn't begun yet, collapse is imminent. At the conference in Hilo, Kevin Higgins of the University of Oregon presented a computer model that tracks artificial organisms in a population, simulating their genetic mutation rates, reproductive behavior and ecological interactions. He found that "in small populations, mutations tend to be mild enough that natural selection doesn't filter them out. That dramatically shortens the time to extinction." So as habitats shrink and populations are wiped out—at a rate of perhaps 16 million a year, Daily has estimated— "this could be a time bomb, an extinction event occurring under the surface," Higgins warns. But proving that that bomb is ticking in the wild will not be easy.

And what will happen to fig trees, the most widespread plant genus in the tropics, if it loses the single parasitic wasp variety that pollinates every one of its 900 species? Or to the 79 percent of canopy-level trees in the Samoan rain forests if hunters kill off the flying foxes on which they depend? Part of the reason so many conservationists are so fearful is that they expect the arches of entire ecosystems to fall once a few "keystone" species are removed.

Others distrust that metaphor. "Several recent studies seem to show that there is some redundancy in ecosystems," says Melodie A. McGeoch of the University of Pretoria in South Africa, although she cautions that what is redundant today may not be redundant tomorrow. "It really doesn't make sense to think the majority of species would go down with marginally higher pressures than if humans weren't on the scene," MacPhee adds. "Evolution should make them resilient."

If natural selection doesn't do so, artificial selection might, according to work by Werner Greuter of the Free University of Berlin, Thomas M. Brooks of Conservation International and others. Greuter compared the rate of recent plant extinctions in four ecologically similar regions and discovered that the longest-settled, most disturbed area—the Mediterranean—had the lowest rate. Plant extinction rates were higher in California and South Africa, and they were highest in Western Australia. The solution to this apparent paradox, they propose, is that species that cannot coexist with human land use tend to die out soon after agriculture begins. Those that are left are better equipped to dodge the darts we throw at them. Human-induced extinctions may thus fall over time.

If true, that has several implications. Millennia ago our ancestors may have killed off many more species than we care to think about in Europe, Asia and other long-settled regions. On the other hand, we may have more time than we fear to prevent future catastrophes in areas where humans have been part of the ecosystem for a while—and less time than we hope to avoid them in what little wilderness remains pristine.

"The question is how to deal with uncertainty, because there really is no way to make that uncertainty go away," Winemiller argues. "We think the situation is extremely serious; we just don't think the species extinction issue is the peg the conservation movement should hang its hat on. Otherwise, if it turns out to be wrong, where does that leave us?"

Long-Term Savings

It could leave conservationists with less of a sense of urgency and with a handful of weak political and economic arguments. It might also force them to realize that "many of the species in trouble today are in fact

continued on page 136

Why Biodiversity Doesn't (Yet) Pay

FOZ DO IGUAÇU, BRAZIL—At the International Congress of
Entomologists last summer, Ebbe Nielsen, director of the
Australian National Insect Collection in Canberra,
reflected on the reasons why, despite the 1992
Convention of Biological Diversity signed here in Brazil
by 178 countries, so little has happened since to secure
the world's threatened species. "You and I can say
extinction rates are too high and we have to stop it, but
to convince the politicians we have to have convincing
reasons," he said. "In developing countries, the economic
pressures are so high, people use whatever they can
find today to survive until tomorrow. As long as that's the
case, there will be no support for biodiversity at all."

Not, that is, unless it can be made more profitable
to leave a forest standing or a wetland wet than it is to
convert the land to farm, pasture or parking lot.
Unfortunately, time has not been kind to the several
arguments environmentalists have made to assign economic value to each one of perhaps 10 million species.

A Hedge Against Disease and Famine

"Narrowly utilitarian arguments say: The incredible
genetic diversity contained in the population and
species diversity that we are heirs to is ultimately the
raw stuff of tomorrow's biotechnological revolution,"
observes Robert May of Oxford. "It is the source of new
drugs." Or new foods, adds E. O. Wilson of Harvard, should

something happen to the 30 crops that supply 90 percent of the calories to the human diet, or to the 14 animal species that make up 90 percent of our livestock.

"Some people who say that may even believe it," May continues. "I don't. Give us 20 or 30 years and we will design new drugs from the molecule up, as we are already beginning to do."

Hopes were raised 10 years ago by reports that Merck had paid $1.14 million to InBio, a Costa Rican conservation group, for novel chemicals extracted from rain-forest species. The contract would return royalties to InBio if any of the leads became drugs. But none have, and Merck terminated the agreement in 1999. Shaman Pharmaceuticals, founded in 1989 to commercialize traditional medicinal plants, got as far as late-stage clinical trials but then went bankrupt. And given, as Wilson himself notes in *The Diversity of Life*, that more than 90 percent of the known varieties of the basic food plants are on deposit in seed banks, national parks are hardly the cheapest form of insurance against crop failures.

Ecosystem Services

"Potentially the strongest argument," May says, "is a broadly utilitarian one: ecological systems deliver services we're only just beginning to think of trying to estimate. We do not understand how much you can simplify these systems and yet still have them function.

continued on following page

continued from previous page

As Aldo Leopold once said, the first rule of intelligent tinkering is to keep all the pieces."

The trouble with this argument, explains Columbia University economist Geoffrey Heal, is that "it does not make sense to ask about the value of replacing a life-support system." Economics can only assign the value to things for which there are markets, he says. If all oil were to vanish, for example, we could switch to alternative fuels that cost $50 a barrel. But that does not determine the price of oil.

And although recent experiments suggest that removing a large fraction of species from a small area lowers its biomass and ability to soak up carbon dioxide, scientists cannot say yet whether the principle applies to whole ecosystems. "It may be that a grievously simplified world—the world of the cult movie *Blade Runner*—can be so run that we can survive in it," May concedes.

A Duty of Stewardship

Because science knows so little of the millions of species out there, let alone what complex roles each one plays in the ecosystems it inhabits, it may never be possible for economics to come to the aid of endangered species. A moral argument may thus be the best last hope—certainly it is appeals to leaders' sense of stewardship that have accomplished the most so far. But is it hazardous for scientists to make it?

They do, of course, in various forms. To Wilson, "a species is a masterpiece of evolution, a million-year-old entity encoded by five billion genetic letters, exquisitely adapted to the niche it inhabits." For that reason, conservation biologist David Ehrenfeld proposed in *The Arrogance of Humanism*, "long-standing existence in Nature is deemed to carry with it the unimpeachable right to continued existence."

Winning public recognition of such a right will take much education and persuasion. According to a poll last year, fewer than one quarter of Americans recognized the term "biological diversity." Three quarters expressed concern about species and habitat loss, but that is down from 87 percent in 1996. And May observes that the concept of biodiversity stewardship "is a developed-world luxury. If we were in abject poverty trying to put food in the mouth of the fifth child, the argument would have less resonance."

But if scientists "proselytize on behalf of biodiversity"— as Wilson, Lovejoy, Ehrlich and many others have done— they should realize that "such work carries perils," advises David Takacs of California State University at Monterey Bay. "Advocacy threatens to undermine the perception of value neutrality and objectivity that leads laypersons to listen to scientists in the first place." And yet if those who know rare species best and love them most cannot speak openly on their behalf, who will?

continued from page 131

already members of the doomed, living dead," as David S. Woodruff wrote in the *Proceedings of the National Academy of Sciences* this past May. "Triage" is a dirty word to many environmentalists. "Unless we say no species loss is acceptable, then we have no line in the sand to defend, and we will be pushed back and back as losses build," Brooks argued at the Hilo meeting. But losses are inevitable, Wilson says, until the human population stops growing.

"I call that the bottleneck," Wilson elaborates, "because we have to pass through that scramble for remaining resources in order to get to an era, perhaps sometime in the 22nd century, of declining population. Our goal is to carry as much of the biodiversity through as possible." Biologists are divided, however, on whether the few charismatic species now recognized as endangered should determine what gets pulled through the bottleneck.

"The argument that when you protect birds and mammals, the other things come with them just doesn't stand up to close examination," May says. A smarter goal is "to try to conserve the greatest amount of evolutionary history." Far more valuable than a panda or rhino, he suggests, are relic life-forms such as the tuatara, a large iguana-like reptile that lives only on islets off the coast of New Zealand. Just two species of tuatara remain from a group that branched off from the main stem of the reptilian evolutionary tree so long ago that this couple make up a genus, an order and almost a subclass all by themselves.

But Woodruff, who is an ecologist at the University of California at San Diego, invokes an even broader principle. "Some of us advocate a shift from saving things, the products of evolution, to saving the underlying process, evolution itself," he writes. "This process will ultimately provide us with the most cost-effective solution to the general problem of conserving nature."

There are still a few large areas where natural selection alone determines which species succeed and which fail. "Why not save functioning ecosystems that haven't been despoiled yet?" Winemiller asks. "Places like the Guyana shield region of South America contain far more species than some of the so-called hotspots." To do so would mean purchasing tracts large enough to accommodate entire ecosystems as they roll north and south in response to the shifting climate. It would also mean prohibiting all human uses of the land. It may not be impossible: utterly undeveloped wilderness is relatively cheap, and the population of potential buyers has recently exploded.

"It turns out to be a lot easier to persuade a corporate CEO or a billionaire of the importance of the issue than it is to convince the American public," Wilson says. "With a Ted Turner or a Gordon Moore or a Craig McCaw involved, you can accomplish almost as much as a government of a developed country would with a fairly generous appropriation."

"Maybe even more," agrees Richard E. Rice, chief economist for Conservation International. With money from Moore, McCaw, Turner and other donors, CI has outcompeted logging companies for forested land in Suriname and Guyana. In Bolivia, Rice reports, "we conserved an area the size of Rhode Island for half the price of a house in my neighborhood," and the Nature Conservancy was able to have a swath of rain forest as big as Yellowstone National Park set aside for a mere $1.5 million. In late July, Peru issued to an environmental group the country's first "conservation concession"—essentially a renewable lease for the right to not develop the land—for 130,000 hectares of forest. Peru has now opened some 60 million hectares of its public forests to such concessions, Rice says. And efforts are under way to negotiate similar deals in Guatemala and Cameroon.

"Even without massive support in public opinion or really effective government policy in the U.S., things are turning upward," Wilson says, with a look of cautious optimism on his face. Perhaps it is a bit early to despair after all.

W. Wayt Gibbs is senior writer.

3 Human Impacts

The preceding articles have touched on issues pertaining to human population growth, but that issue is the main focus of this next piece. From the human standpoint, it is hard to see population growth as negative. After all, who wants to be the one to leave the planet to lower our numbers? Still, the reality is that our ever-rising population is changing our lives and the lives of all other beings on Earth. The swelling population will directly affect your future.

People are living longer, and there are more of us. Although individuals may live to become senior citizens, they may no longer be able to work and to take care of themselves. Many diseases, such as Alzheimer's and Parkinson's, are often linked to aging, so, in the future, someone is going to have to pay the bill for the care of the elderly. With social security programs forever on governmental chopping blocks, societies may be unable to look after their elderly. Since you could be one such person, the issue is worth considering even now. The following article also touches upon potential problems related to food availability,

violence, and poverty, which will be discussed in
more detail in the rest of this chapter. —JV

"Human Population Grows Up"
by Joel E. Cohen
Scientific American, September 2005

The year 2005 is the midpoint of a decade that spans
three unique, important transitions in the history of
humankind. Before 2000, young people always outnumbered old people. From 2000 forward, old people
will outnumber young people. Until approximately
2007, rural people will have always outnumbered
urban people. From approximately 2007 forward, urban
people will outnumber rural people. From 2003 on,
the median woman worldwide had, and will continue
to have, too few or just enough children during her
lifetime to replace herself and the father in the following
generation.

The century with 2000 as its midpoint marks three
additional unique, important transitions in human
history. First, no person who died before 1930 had
lived through a doubling of the human population. Nor
is any person born in 2050 or later likely to live through
a doubling of the human population. In contrast,
everyone 45 years old or older today has seen more
than a doubling of human numbers from three billion
in 1960 to 6.5 billion in 2005. The peak population
growth rate ever reached, about 2.1 percent a year,
occurred between 1965 and 1970. Human population

never grew with such speed before the 20th century and is never again likely to grow with such speed. Our descendants will look back on the late 1960s peak as the most significant demographic event in the history of the human population even though those of us who lived through it did not recognize it at the time.

Second, the dramatic fall since 1970 of the global population growth rate to 1.1 or 1.2 percent a year today resulted primarily from choices by billions of couples around the world to limit the number of children born. Global human population growth rates have probably risen and fallen numerous times in the past. The great plagues and wars of the 14th century, for example, reduced not only the growth rate but also the absolute size of global population, both largely involuntary changes. Never before the 20th century has a fall in the global population growth rate been voluntary.

Finally, the last half a century saw, and the next half a century will see, an enormous shift in the demographic balance between the more developed regions of the world and the less developed ones. Whereas in 1950 the less developed regions had roughly twice the population of the more developed ones, by 2050 the ratio will exceed six to one.

These colossal changes in the composition and dynamics of the human population by and large escape public notice. Occasionally, one or another symptom of these profound shifts does attract political attention. Proposed Social Security reforms in the U.S., however, often fail to recognize the fundamental population aging, while debates in Europe and the U.S. over immigration policy often overlook the differences in population growth rates between these regions and their southern neighbors.

In this article, I will focus on the four major underlying trends expected to dominate changes in the human population in the coming half-century and some of their long-term implications. The population will be bigger, slower-growing, more urban, and older than in the 20th century. Of course, precise projections remain highly uncertain. Small changes in assumed fertility rates have enormous effects on the projected total numbers of people, for example. Despite such caveats, the projections do suggest some of the problems that humanity will have to face over the next 50 years.

Rapid but Slowing Growth

Although the rate of population growth has fallen since the 1970s, the logic of compounding means that current levels of global population growth are still greater than any experienced prior to World War II. Whereas the first absolute increase in population by one billion people took from the beginning of time until the early 19th century, one billion people will be added to today's population in only 13 to 14 years. By 2050 the world's population is projected to reach 9.1 billion, plus or minus two billion people, depending on future birth and death rates. This anticipated increase of 2.6 billion people by 2050 over the 6.5 billion people

Crossroads for Population

The Problem:

- Rapid population growth will boost human numbers by nearly 50 percent, from 6.5 billion now to 9.1 billion in 2050. Virtually all this growth will happen in existing or new cities in developing countries. During the same period, many richer nations will lose population. Falling fertility and increasing longevity worldwide will expand the proportion of potentially dependent elderly people.

The Plan:

- Create a bigger pie, and fewer forks, and better manners: Intensify human productive capacity through investment in education, health and technology. Increase access to reproductive health care and contraception to voluntarily slow population growth. Improve the terms of people's interactions by reforming economic, political, civil and social institutions, policies and practices and achieving greater social and legal equity.

of 2005 exceeds the total population of the world in 1950, which was 2.5 billion.

In short, rapid population growth has not ended. Human numbers currently increase by 74 million to 76 million people annually, the equivalent of adding another U.S. to the world every four years. But most of the increases are not occurring in countries with the wealth of the U.S. Between 2005 and 2050 population will at least triple in Afghanistan, Burkina Faso, Burundi, Chad, Congo, Democratic Republic of the Congo, East Timor, Guinea-Bissau, Liberia, Mali, Niger and Uganda. These countries are among the poorest on Earth.

Virtually all population growth in the next 45 years is expected to happen in today's economically less developed regions. Despite higher death rates at every age, poor countries' populations grow faster than rich countries' populations because birth rates in poor countries are much higher. At present, the average woman bears nearly twice as many children (2.9) in the poor countries as in the rich countries (1.6 children per woman).

Half the global increase will be accounted for by just nine nations. Listed in order of their anticipated contribution, they are India, Pakistan, Nigeria, Democratic Republic of the Congo, Bangladesh, Uganda, the U.S., Ethiopia and China. The only rich country on the list is the U.S., where roughly one third of population growth is driven by a high rate of immigration [*see box on page 150*].

In contrast, 51 countries or areas, most of them economically more developed, will lose population between now and 2050. Germany is expected to drop from 83 million to 79 million people, Italy from 58 million to 51 million, Japan from 128 million to 112 million and, most dramatically, the Russian Federation from 143 million to 112 million. Thereafter Russia will be slightly smaller in population than Japan.

Slowing population growth everywhere means that the 20th century was probably the last in human history in which younger people outnumbered older ones. The proportion of all people who were children aged four years and younger peaked in 1955 at 14.5 percent and gradually declined to 9.5 percent by 2005, whereas the fraction of people aged 60 years and older increased from a low of 8.1 percent in 1960 to 10.4 percent in 2005. Around 2000 each group constituted about 10 percent of humanity. Now and henceforth the elderly have the numerical upper hand.

This crossover in the proportions of young and old reflects both improved survival and reduced fertility. The average life span grew from perhaps 30 years at the beginning of the 20th century to more than 65 years at the beginning of the 21st century. The more powerful influence, however, is reduced fertility, adding smaller numbers to the younger age groups.

The graying of the population is not proceeding uniformly around the globe. In 2050 nearly one person in three will be 60 years or older in the more developed regions and one person in five in the less developed zones. But in 11 of the least developed countries— Afghanistan, Angola, Burundi, Chad, Democratic Republic of the Congo, Equatorial Guinea, Guinea-Bissau, Liberia, Mali, Niger and Uganda—half the population will be aged 23 years or younger.

If recent trends continue as projected to 2050, virtually all of the world's population growth will be in urban areas. In effect, the poor countries will have to build the equivalent of a city of more than one million people each week for the next 45 years.

Although long-term demographic projections to 2050 and beyond are routine, economic models are not well developed for long-term projection. They are vulnerable to unpredictable changes in institutions and technology and to shifts in the dominance of regions and economic sectors. Most models do, however, predict that the world will become richer. In the brightest scenarios, the ratio of per capita income in industrial nations to that in developing nations could drop from an estimated 16 to 1 in 1990 to between 6.6 to 1 and 2.8 to 1 in 2050. These gains are not assured. Other models predict stagnating poverty.

Projections of billions more people in developing countries and more elderly people everywhere, coupled with hopes of economic growth especially for the world's poor, raise concerns in some quarters about the sustainability of present and future populations.

Beyond Human Carrying Capacity

In the short term, our planet can provide room and food, at least at a subsistence level, for 50 percent more people than are alive now because humans are already growing enough cereal grains to feed 10 billion people a vegetarian diet. But as demographer-sociologist Kingsley Davis observed in 1991, "There is no country in the world in which people are satisfied with having barely enough to eat." The question is whether 2050's billions of people can live with freedom of choice and material prosperity, however freedom and prosperity may be defined by those alive in 2050, and whether their children and their children's offspring will be able to continue to live with freedom and prosperity, however they may define them in the future. That is the question of sustainability.

This worry is as old as recorded history. Cuneiform tablets from 1600 BC showed that the Babylonians feared the world was already too full of people. In 1798 Thomas Malthus renewed these concerns, as did Donella Meadows in her 1972 book *The Limits to Growth*. While some people have fretted about too many people, optimists have offered reassurance that deities or technology will provide for humankind's well-being.

Early efforts to calculate Earth's human carrying capacity assumed that a necessary condition for a sustainable human society could be measured in units of land. In the first known quantitative reckoning, Antoni van Leeuwenhoek estimated in 1679 that the inhabited area of Earth was 13,385 times larger than Holland and that Holland's population then was about one million people. Assuming that "the inhabited part of the earth is as densely populated as Holland, though it cannot well be so inhabited," he wrote, "the inhabited earth being 13,385 times larger than Holland yields . . . 13,385,000,000 human beings on the earth," or an upper limit of roughly 13.4 billion.

Continuing this tradition, in 2002 Mathis Wackernagel, an author of the "ecological footprint" concept, and his colleagues sought to quantify the amount of land humans used to supply resources and to absorb wastes. Their preliminary assessment concluded that humanity used 70 percent of the global biosphere's capacity in 1961 and 120 percent in 1999. In other words, by 1999 people were exploiting the environment faster than it could regenerate itself, they claimed, a situation that is clearly unsustainable.

This approach has many problems. Perhaps the most serious is its attempt to establish a necessary condition for the sustainability of human society in terms of the single dimension of biologically productive land area. For instance, to translate energy use into land units, Wackernagel and his colleagues calculated the area of forests that would be needed to absorb the carbon dioxide produced in generating the energy. This approach fails for energy generation technologies that do not emit carbon dioxide, such as solar panels, hydropower or nuclear plants. Converting all energy production to nuclear energy would change the dilemma from too much CO_2 to too much spent nuclear fuel. The problem of sustainability remains, but biologically productive land area is not a useful indicator of it.

Other one-dimensional quantities that have been proposed as ceilings on human carrying capacity include water, energy, food and various chemical elements required for food production. The difficulty with every single index of human carrying capacity is that its meaning depends on the value of other factors. If water is scarce and energy is abundant, for example, it is easy to desalinate and transport water; if energy is expensive, desalination and transport may be impractical.

Attempts to quantify Earth's human carrying capacity or a sustainable human population size face the challenge of understanding the constraints imposed by nature, the choices faced by people and the interactions between them. Some of the constraints imposed by nature are dealt with elsewhere in this issue. Here I will draw attention to the questions of human choice involved in assessing sustainability.

What will humans desire and what will they accept as the average level and distribution of material well-being in 2050 and beyond? What technologies will be used? What domestic and international political institutions will be used to resolve conflicts? What economic arrangements will provide credit, regulate trade, set standards and fund investments? What social and demographic arrangements will influence birth, health, education, marriage, migration and death? What physical, chemical and biological environments will people want to live in? What level of variability will people be willing to live with? (If people do not mind seeing human population size drop by billions when the climate becomes unfavorable, they may regard a much larger population as sustainable when the climate is favorable.) What level of risk are people willing to live with? (Are mud slides, hurricanes or floods acceptable risks or not? The answer will influence the

The Migration Wild Card

Migration has little immediate effect on global population size but may accelerate the slowing of population growth. Migrants who move from high-fertility to low-fertility regions or their descendants often adopt the reduced-fertility patterns of their new home, with some time delay. From 2005 to 2050, the more developed regions are projected to have about 2.2 million more immigrants than emigrants a year, and the U.S. is expected to receive about half of these.

More than most demographic variables, future international migration is subject to intentional policy choices by national governments, making it difficult to predict. Assuming that recent levels of migration continue, the 98 million net migrants expected to move to the developed regions during 2005–2050 would more than offset the projected loss of 73 million people in those countries from an excess of deaths over births. Different international migration scenarios would not greatly affect the sharp rise in the rich countries' proportion of dependent elderly projected for the coming century, although they could dramatically affect population size.

In 2000, for example, the U.S. Census Bureau projected the nation's numbers in 2050 with different levels of immigration. Results ranged from 328 million, representing a 20 percent population increase with zero immigration, to 553 million, representing an 80 percent increase with the highest level of immigration—hypothetical net annual immigration rising to 2.8 million by 2050. Regardless of migration, though, the U.S. ratio of elderly to working-age people will rise steeply from 2010 until around 2035 and will gradually increase thereafter. By 2050 it is projected to reach 39 percent with zero immigration and 30 percent with the highest immigration.   —*J. E. C.*

area of land viewed as habitable.) What time horizon is assumed? Finally, and significantly, what will people's values and tastes be in the future? As anthropologist Donald L. Hardesty noted in 1977, "A plot of land may have a low carrying capacity, not because of low soil fertility but because it is sacred or inhabited by ghosts."

Most published estimates of Earth's human carrying capacity uncritically assumed answers to one or more of these questions. In my book *How Many People Can the Earth Support?* I collected and analyzed more than five dozen of these estimates published from 1679 onward. Those made in just the past half a century ranged from less than one billion to more than 1,000 billion. These estimates are political numbers, intended to persuade people, one way or another: either that too many humans are already on Earth or that there is no problem with continuing rapid population growth.

Scientific numbers are intended to describe reality. Because no estimates of human carrying capacity have explicitly addressed the questions raised above, taking into account the diversity of views about their answers in different societies and cultures, no scientific estimates of sustainable human population size can be said to exist.

Too often attention to long-term sustainability is a diversion from the immediate problem of making tomorrow better than today, a task that does offer much room for science and constructive action. Let us therefore briefly consider two major demographic trends, urbanization and aging, and some of the choices they present.

Boom or Bomb?

Many major cities were established in regions of exceptional agricultural productivity, typically the floodplains of rivers, or in coastal zones and islands with favorable access to marine food resources and maritime commerce. If the world's urban population roughly doubles in the next half a century, from three billion to six billion, while the world's rural population remains roughly constant at three billion, and if many cities expand in area rather than increasing in density, fertile agricultural lands around those cities could be removed from production, and the waters around coastal or island cities could face a growing challenge from urban waste.

Right now the most densely settled half of the planet's population lives on 2 to 3 percent of all ice-free land. If cities double in area as well as population by 2050, urban areas could grow to occupy 6 percent of land. Withdrawing that amount mostly from the 10 to 15 percent of land considered arable could have a notable impact on agricultural production. Planning cities to avoid consuming arable land would greatly reduce the effect of their population growth on food production, a goal very much in the urbanites' interest because the cities will need to be provisioned.

Unless urban food gardening surges, on average each rural person will have to shift from feeding herself (most of the world's agricultural workers are women) and one city dweller today to feeding herself and two urbanites in less than half a century. If the intensity of rural agricultural production increases, the demand for food, along with the technology supplied by the growing cities to the rural regions, may ultimately lift the rural agrarian population from poverty, as happened in many rich countries. On the other hand, if more chemical fertilizers and biocides are applied to raise yields, the rise in food production could put huge strains on the environment.

For city dwellers, urbanization threatens frightening hazards from infectious disease unless adequate sanitation measures supply clean water and remove wastes. Yet cities also concentrate opportunities for educational and cultural enrichment, access to health care, and diverse employment. Therefore, if half the urban infrastructure that will exist in the world of 2050 must be built in the next 45 years, the opportunity to design, construct, operate and maintain new cities better than old ones is enormous, exciting and challenging.

Urbanization will interact with the transformation of human societies by aging. Cities raise the economic premium paid to younger, better-educated workers whereas the mobility they promote often weakens traditional kin networks that provide familial support to elderly people. An older, uneducated woman who could have familial support and productive work in agriculture if she lived in a rural area might have difficulty finding both a livelihood and social support in a city.

After 2010, most countries will experience a sharp acceleration in the rate of increase of the elderly dependency ratio—the ratio of the number of people aged 65 and older to the number aged 15 to 64. The shift will come first and most acutely in the more developed countries, whereas the least developed countries will experience a slow increase in elderly dependency after 2020. By 2050 the elderly dependency ratio of the least developed countries will approach that of the more developed countries in 1950.

Extrapolating directly from age to economic and social burdens is unreliable, however. The economic burden imposed by elderly people will depend on their health, on the economic institutions available to offer them work, and on the social institutions on hand to support their care.

Trends in the health of the elderly are positive overall, despite severe problems in some economies in transition and regions afflicted by AIDS. The rate of chronic disability among elderly Americans, for example, declined rapidly between 1982 and 1999. As a result, by 1999, 25 percent fewer elderly Americans were chronically disabled than would have been expected if the U.S. disability rate had remained constant since 1982.

Because an older person relies first on his or her spouse in case of difficulty (if there is a spouse), marital status is also a key influence on living conditions among the elderly. Married elderly people are more likely to be maintained at home rather than institutionalized compared with single, widowed or divorced persons.

The sustainability of the elderly population depends in complex ways not only on age, gender and marital status but also on the availability of supportive offspring and on socioeconomic status—notably educational attainment. Better education in youth is associated with better health in old age. Consequently, one obvious strategy to improve the sustainability of the coming wave of older people is to invest in educating youth today, including education in those behaviors that preserve health and promote the stability of marriage. Another obvious strategy is to invest in the economic and social institutions that facilitate economic productivity and social engagement among elderly people.

No one knows the path to sustainability because no one knows the destination, if there is one. But we do know much that we could do today to make tomorrow better than it would be if we do not put our knowledge to work. As economist Robert Cassen remarked, "Virtually everything that needs doing from a population point of view needs doing anyway."

The Author

Joel E. Cohen is Professor of Populations and head of the Laboratory of Populations at the Rockefeller University and Columbia University. He studies the population biology, demography, ecology and epidemiology of human and nonhuman populations using mathematics, statistics and computation. Author, co-author or editor of a dozen books and author of more than 320 papers, he has won the Tyler Prize for Environmental Achievement, the Nordberg Prize for excellence in writing in the population sciences, and the Fred L. Soper Prize of the Pan American Health Organization for his work on Chagas' disease. He enjoys playing the piano and being father to "the two best children in the world."

Based on current patterns, populations are expected to soar in some of the world's poorest regions, such as central and eastern Africa and western and southern Asia. Author Partha Dasgupta, who was educated in both India and Britain, provides an enlightened perspective on the issue of population growth in the next article. He suggests that lack of education may prevent individuals, and particularly women, from making

*informed decisions about having children.
Further complicating the matter is the traditional
view in some countries that more children
means that a larger workforce will be available
to support the family. In practice, that tradition
is often disadvantageous, especially for the
children. In Mumbai, the largest city in India,
poor children often must sleep in the streets,
where they beg and band together for survival.
If they do survive, they usually are not able to
go to school. When they reach childbearing age,
the vicious pattern may start all over again,
unless family planning services and other possible
solutions break the cycle. —JV*

"Population, Poverty and the Local Environment"
by Partha S. Dasgupta
Scientific American, February 1995

As with politics, we all have widely differing opinions
about population. Some would point to population
growth as the cause of poverty and environmental
degradation. Others would permute the elements of
this causal chain, arguing, for example, that poverty is
the cause rather than the consequence of increasing
numbers. Yet even when studying the semi-arid regions
of sub-Saharan Africa and the Indian subcontinent,
economists have typically not regarded poverty,
population growth and the local environment as

interconnected. Inquiry into each factor has in large measure gone along its own narrow route, with discussion of their interactions dominated by popular writings—which, although often illuminating, are in the main descriptive and not analytical.

Over the past several years, though, a few investigators have studied the relations between these ingredients more closely. Our approach fuses theoretical modeling with empirical findings drawn from a number of disciplines, such as anthropology, demography, ecology, economics, nutrition and political science. Focusing on the vast numbers of small, rural communities in the poorest regions of the world, the work has identified circumstances in which population growth, poverty and degradation of local resources often fuel one another. The collected research has shown that none of the three elements directly causes the other two; rather each influences, and is in turn influenced by, the others. This new perspective has significant implications for policies aimed at improving life for some of the world's most impoverished inhabitants.

In contrast with this new perspective, with its focus on local experience, popular tracts on the environment and population growth have usually taken a global view. They have emphasized the deleterious effects that a large population would have on our planet in the distant future. Although that slant has its uses, it has drawn attention away from the economic misery endemic today. Disaster is not something the poorest have to wait for: it is occurring even now. Besides, in developing countries, decisions on whether to have a child and on how to share education, food, work, health care and local resources are in large measure made within small entities such as households. So it makes sense to study the link between poverty, population growth and the environment from a myriad of local, even individual, viewpoints.

The household assumes various guises in different parts of the world. Some years ago Gary S. Becker of the University of Chicago was the first investigator to grapple with this difficulty. He used an idealized version of the concept to explore how choices made within a household would respond to changes in the outside world, such as employment opportunities and availability of credit, insurance, health care and education.

One problem with his method, as I saw it when I began my own work some five years ago, was that it studied households in isolation; it did not investigate the dynamics between interacting units. In addition to understanding the forces that encouraged couples to favor large families, I wanted to understand the ways in which a reasoned decision to have children, made by each household, could end up being detrimental to all households.

In studying how such choices are made, I found a second problem with the early approach: by assuming that decision making was shared equally by adults, investigators had taken an altogether too benign view of the process. Control over a family's choices is, after all, often held unequally. If I wanted to understand how decisions were made, I would have to know who was doing the deciding.

Power and Gender

Those who enjoy the greatest power within a family can often be identified by the way the household's resources are divided. Judith Bruce of the Population Council, Mayra Buvinic of the International Center for Research on Women, Lincoln C. Chen and Amartya Sen of Harvard University and others have observed that the sharing of resources within a household is often unequal even when differences in needs are taken into account. In poor households in the Indian subcontinent, for example, men and boys usually get more sustenance than do women and girls, and the elderly get less than the young.

Such inequities prevail over fertility choices as well. Here also men wield more influence, even though women typically bear the greater cost. To grasp how great the burden can be, consider the number of live babies a woman would normally have if she managed to survive through her childbearing years. This number, called the total fertility rate, is between six and eight in sub-Saharan Africa. Each successful birth there involves at least a year and a half of pregnancy and breast-feeding. So in a society where female life expectancy at birth is 50 years and the fertility rate is, say, seven, nearly half of a woman's adult life is spent either carrying a child in her womb or breast-feeding it.

Total fertility rate around the world (the average number of children a woman produces) generally increases with the percentage of women in a country who are illiterate (*top*) or work unpaid in the family (*middle*). Fertility decreases when a larger share of the paid employment belongs to women (*bottom*). Bringing in a cash income may empower a woman in making decisions within her family, allowing her to resist pressure to bear more children.

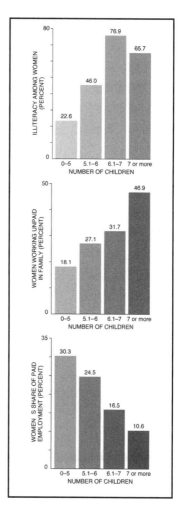

And this calculation does not allow for unsuccessful pregnancies.

Another indicator of the price that women pay is maternal mortality. In most poor countries, complications related to pregnancy constitute the largest single cause of death of women in their reproductive years. In some parts of sub-Saharan Africa as many as one woman dies for every 50 live births. (The rate in Scandinavia today is one per 20,000.) At a total fertility rate of seven or more, the chance that a woman entering her reproductive years will not live through them is about one in six. Producing children therefore involves playing a kind of Russian roulette.

Given such a high cost of procreation, one expects that women, given a choice, would opt for fewer children. But are birth rates in fact highest in societies where women have the least power within the family? Data on the status of women from 79 so-called Third World countries display an unmistakable pattern: high fertility, high rates of illiteracy, low share of paid employment and a high percentage working at home for no pay—they all hang together. From the statistics alone it is difficult to discern which of these factors are causing, and which are merely correlated with, high fertility. But the findings are consistent with the possibility that lack of paid employment and education limits a woman's ability to make decisions and therefore promotes population growth.

There is also good reason to think that lack of income-generating employment reduces women's power more directly than does lack of education. Such an insight has implications for policy. It is all well and good, for example, to urge governments in poor countries to invest in literacy programs. But the results could be disappointing. Many factors militate against poor households' taking advantage of subsidized education. If children are needed to work inside and outside the home, then keeping them in school (even a cheap one) is costly. In patrilineal societies, educated girls can also be perceived as less pliable and harder to marry off. Indeed, the benefits of subsidies to even primary education are reaped disproportionately by families that are better off.

In contrast, policies aimed at increasing women's productivity at home and improving their earnings in the marketplace would directly empower them, especially within the family. Greater earning power for women would also raise for men the implicit costs of procreation (which keeps women from bringing in cash income). This is not to deny the value of public investment in primary and secondary education in developing countries. It is only to say we should be wary of claims that such investment is a panacea for the population problem.

The importance of gender inequality to over-population in poor nations is fortunately gaining international recognition. Indeed, the United Nations Conference on Population and Development held in Cairo in September 1994 emphasized women's repro-ductive rights and the means by which they could be protected and promoted. But there is more to the population problem than gender inequalities. Even when both parents participate in the decision to have a child, there are several pathways through which the choice becomes harmful to the community. These routes have been uncovered by inquiring into the various motives for procreation.

Little Hands Help . . .

One motive, common to humankind, relates to children as ends in themselves. It ranges from the desire to have children because they are playful and enjoyable, to the desire to obey the dictates of tradition and religion. One such injunction emanates from the cult of the ancestor, which, taking religion to be the act of reproducing the lineage, requires women to bear many children.

Such traditions are often perpetuated by imitative behavior. Procreation in closely knit communities is not only a private matter; it is also a social activity, influenced by the cultural milieu. Often there are norms encouraging high fertility rates that no household desires unilaterally to break. (These norms may well have outlasted any rationale they had in the past.) Consequently, so long as all others aim at large families, no household on its own will wish to deviate. Thus, a society can get stuck at a self-sustaining mode of behavior that is characterized by high fertility and low educational attainment.

This does not mean that society will live with it forever. As always, people differ in the extent to which they adhere to tradition. Inevitably some, for one reason or another, will experiment, take risks and refrain from joining the crowd. They are the nonconformists, and they help to lead the way. An increase in female literacy could well trigger such a process.

Still other motives for procreation involve viewing children as productive assets. In a rural economy where avenues for saving are highly restricted, parents value children as a source of security in their old age. Mead Cain, previously at the Population Council, studied this aspect extensively. Less discussed, at least until recently, is another kind of motivation, explored by John C. Caldwell of the Australian National University, Marc L. Nerlove of the University of Maryland and Anke S. Meyer of the World Bank and by Karl-Göran Mäler of the Beijer International Institute of Ecological Economics in Stockholm and me. It stems from children's being valuable to their parents not only for future income but also as a source of current income.

Third World countries are, for the most part, subsistence economies. The rural folk eke out a living by using products gleaned directly from plants and animals. Much labor is needed even for simple tasks. In addition, poor rural households do not have access to modern sources of domestic energy or tap water. In semi-arid and arid regions the water supply may not even be nearby. Nor is fuel wood at hand when the forests recede. In addition to cultivating crops, caring for livestock, cooking food and producing simple marketable products, members of a household may have to spend as much as five to six hours a day fetching water and collecting fodder and wood.

Children, then, are needed as workers even when their parents are in their prime. Small households are simply not viable; each one needs many hands. In parts of India, children between 10 and 15 years have been observed to work as much as one and a half times the number of hours that adult males do. By the age of six, children in rural India tend domestic animals and care for younger siblings, fetch water and collect firewood, dung and fodder. It may well be that the usefulness of each extra hand increases with declining availability of resources, as measured by, say, the distance to sources of fuel and water.

... But at a Hidden Cost

The need for many hands can lead to a destructive situation, especially when parents do not have to pay the full price of rearing their children but share those costs with the community. In recent years, mores that once regulated the use of local resources have changed. Since time immemorial, rural assets such as village ponds and water holes, threshing grounds, grazing fields, and local forests have been owned communally. This form of control enabled households in semi-arid regions to pool their risks. Elinor Ostrom of Indiana University and others have shown that communities have protected such local commons against overexploitation by invoking norms, imposing fines for deviant behavior and so forth.

But the very process of economic development can erode traditional methods of control. Increased urbanization and mobility can do so as well. Social rules are also endangered by civil strife and by the takeover of resources by landowners or the state. As norms degrade, parents pass some of the costs of children on to the community by overexploiting the commons. If access to shared resources continues, parents produce too many children, which leads to greater crowding and susceptibility to disease as well as to more pressure on environmental resources. But no household, on its own, takes into account the harm it inflicts on others when bringing forth another child.

Parental costs of procreation are also lower when relatives provide a helping hand. Although the price of carrying a child is paid by the mother, the cost of rearing the child is often shared among the kinship. Caroline H. Bledsoe of Northwestern University and others have observed that in much of sub-Saharan Africa fosterage is commonplace, affording a form of insurance protection in semi-arid regions. In parts of West Africa about a third of the children have been found to be living with their kin at any given time. Nephews and nieces have the same rights of accommodation and support as do biological offspring. In recent work I have shown that this arrangement encourages couples to have too many offspring if the parents' share of the benefits from having children exceeds their share of the costs.

In addition, where conjugal bonds are weak, as they are in sub-Saharan Africa, fathers often do not bear the costs of siring a child. Historical demographers, such as E. A. Wrigley of the University of Cambridge, have noted a significant difference between western Europe in the 18th century and modern preindustrial societies. In the former, marriage normally meant establishing a new household. This requirement led to date marriages; it also meant that parents bore the cost of rearing their children. Indeed, fertility rates in France dropped before mortality rates registered a decline, before modern family-planning techniques became available and before women became literate.

The perception of both the low costs and high benefits of procreation induces households to produce too many children. In certain circumstances a disastrous process can begin. As the community's resources are depleted, more hands are needed to gather fuel and

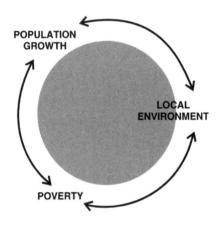

REGION	TOTAL FERTILITY RATE
SUB-SAHARAN AFRICA	6 TO 8
INDIA	4
CHINA	2.3
JAPAN AND WESTERN INDUSTRIAL DEMOCRACIES	1.5 TO 1.9

Poverty, population growth, and environmental degradation interact in a cyclic pattern (*top*). The chart (*bottom*) shows that fertility is higher in countries that are poorer.

water for daily use. More children are then produced, further damaging the local environment and in turn providing the household with an incentive to enlarge. When this happens, fertility and environmental degradation reinforce each other in an escalating spiral. By the time some countervailing set of factors—whether public policy or diminished benefits from having additional children—stops the spiral, millions of lives may have suffered through worsening poverty.

Recent findings by the World Bank on sub-Saharan Africa have revealed positive correlations among poverty, fertility and deterioration of the local environment. Such data cannot reveal causal connections, but they do support the idea of a positive-feedback process such as I have described. Over time, the effect of this spiral can be large, as manifested by battles for resources [see "Environmental Change and Violent Conflict," by T. F. Homer-Dixon, J. H. Boutwell and G. W. Rathjens, on page 174].

The victims hit hardest among those who survive are society's outcasts—the migrants and the dispossessed, some of whom in the course of time become the emaciated beggars seen on the streets of large towns and cities in underdeveloped countries. Historical studies by Robert W. Fogel of the University of Chicago and theoretical explorations by Debraj Ray of Boston University and me, when taken together, show that the spiral I have outlined here is one way in which destitutes are created. Emaciated beggars are not lazy; they have to husband their precarious hold on energy.

Green Net National Production

Some economists believe population growth is conducive to economic growth. They cite statistics showing that, except in sub-Saharan Africa, food production and gross income per head have generally grown since the end of World War II. Even in poor regions, infant survival rate, literacy and life expectancy have improved, despite the population's having grown much faster than in the past.

One weakness of this argument is that it is based on statistics that ignore the depletion of the environmental resource base, on which all production ultimately depends. This base includes soil and its cover, freshwater, breathable air, fisheries and forests. No doubt it is tempting to infer from past trends that human ingenuity can be relied on to overcome the stresses that growing populations impose on the natural environment.

Yet that is not likely to be the case. Societies already use an enormous 40 percent of the net energy created by terrestrial photosynthesis. Geoffrey M. Heal of Columbia University, John M. Hartwick of Queens University and Karl-Göran Mäler of the Beijer International Institute of Ecological Economics in Stockholm and I have shown how to include environmental degradation in estimating the net national product, or NNP. NNP is obtained by deducting from gross national product the value of, for example, coal extracted or timber logged.

This "green NNP" captures not only present production but also the possibility of future production brought about by resources we bequeath. Viewed through NNP, the future appears far less rosy. Indeed, I know of no ecologist who thinks a population of 11 billion (projected for the year 2050) can support itself at a material standard of living of, say, today's representative American.

Having suffered from malnutrition, they cease to be marketable.

Families with greater access to resources are, however, in a position to limit their size and propel themselves into still higher income levels. It is my impression that among the urban middle classes in northern India, the transition to a lower fertility rate has already been achieved. India provides an example of how the vicious cycle I have described can enable extreme poverty to persist amid a growth in well-being in the rest of society. The Matthew effect—"Unto every one that hath shall be given, and he shall have abundance: but from him that hath not shall be taken away even that which he hath"—works relentlessly in impoverished countries.

Breaking Free

This analysis suggests that the way to reduce fertility is to break the destructive spiral. Parental demand for children rather than an unmet need for contraceptives in large measure explains reproductive behavior in developing countries. We should therefore try to identity policies that will change the options available to men and women so that couples choose to limit the number of offspring they produce.

In this regard, civil liberties, as opposed to coercion, play a particular role. Some years ago my colleague Martin R. Weale and I showed through statistical analysis that even in poor countries political and civil liberties go together with improvements in other aspects of life, such as income per person, life expectancy at birth and infant survival rate. Thus, there are now reasons for thinking that such liberties are not only desirable in themselves but also empower people to flourish economically. Recently Adam Przeworski of the University of Chicago demonstrated that fertility, as well, is lower in countries where citizens enjoy more civil and political freedom. (An exception is China, which represents only one country out of many in this analysis.)

The most potent solution in semiarid regions of sub-Saharan Africa and the Indian subcontinent is to deploy a number of policies simultaneously. Family-planning services, especially when allied with health services, and measures that empower women are certainly helpful. As societal norms break down and traditional support systems falter, those women who choose to change their behavior become financially and socially more vulnerable. So a literacy and employment drive for women is essential to smooth the transition to having fewer children.

But improving social coordination and directly increasing the economic security of the poor are also essential. Providing cheap fuel and potable water will reduce the usefulness of extra hands. When a child becomes perceived as expensive, we may finally have a hope of dislodging the rapacious hold of high fertility rates.

Each of the prescriptions suggested by our new perspective on the links between population, poverty and environmental degradation is desirable by itself, not just when we have those problems in mind. It seems to me that this consonance of means and ends is a most agreeable fact in what is otherwise a depressing field of study.

The Author

Partha S. Dasgupta, who was educated in Varanasi, Delhi and Cambridge, is Frank Ramsey Professor of Economics at the University of Cambridge and Fellow of St. John's College. He is also chairman of the Beijer International Institute of Ecological Economics of the Royal Swedish Academy of Sciences in Stockholm and Fellow of the British Academy. Dasgupta's research has ranged over various aspects of environmental, resource and population economics, most recently poverty and malnutrition.

An argument against directing funds toward family planning and environmental protection issues is that more pressing issues, such as global terrorism, require our immediate attention. This next article helps to dispel that argument. It reveals yet another vicious cycle that links inter-group violence with environmental problems.

In the Middle East, for example, rising populations and increasing demand for water caused the water supply to drop in many regions, such as parts of Israel and the West Bank. At this stage, the domino effect began. To ensure that its people would have enough water, the Israeli government restricted use of water in the West Bank, where many Arabs live. That measure hurt local agriculture, so Arabs who used to work as farmers either became unemployed or entered the Israeli job market as day laborers. The resulting problems contributed to tension between Israelis and Arabs in the region. —JV

"Environmental Change and Violent Conflict"
by Thomas F. Homer-Dixon, Jeffrey H. Boutwell, and George W. Rathjens
Scientific American, **February 1993**

Within the next 50 years, the human population is likely to exceed nine billion, and global economic output may quintuple. Largely as a result of these two trends, scarcities of renewable resources may increase sharply. The total area of highly productive agricultural land will drop, as will the extent of forests and the number of species they sustain. Future generations will also experience the ongoing depletion and degradation of aquifers, rivers and other bodies of water, the decline of fisheries, further stratospheric ozone loss and, perhaps, significant climatic change.

As such environmental problems become more severe, they may precipitate civil or international strife. Some concerned scientists have warned of this prospect for several decades, but the debate has been constrained by lack of carefully compiled evidence. To address this shortfall of data, we assembled a team of 30 researchers to examine a set of specific cases. In studies commissioned by the University of Toronto and the American Academy of Arts and Sciences, these experts reported their initial findings.

The evidence that they gathered points to a disturbing conclusion: scarcities of renewable resources are already contributing to violent conflicts in many parts of the developing world. These conflicts may foreshadow a surge of similar violence in coming decades, particularly in poor countries where shortages of water, forests and, especially, fertile land, coupled with rapidly expanding populations, already cause great hardship.

Before we discuss the findings, it is important to note that the environment is but one variable in a series of political, economic and social factors that can bring about turmoil. Indeed, some skeptics claim that scarcities of renewable resources are merely a minor variable that sometimes links existing political and economic factors to subsequent social conflict.

The evidence we have assembled supports a different view [*see illustration on page 180*]. Such scarcity can be an important force behind changes in the politics and economics governing resource use. It can cause powerful actors to strengthen, in their favor, an inequitable distribution of resources. In addition, ecosystem vulnerability often contributes significantly to shortages of renewable resources. This vulnerability is, in part, a physical given: the depth of upland soils in the tropics, for example, is not a function of human social institutions or behavior. And finally, in many parts of the world, environmental degradation seems to have passed a threshold of irreversibility. In these situations, even if enlightened social change removes the original political, economic and cultural causes of the degradation, it may continue to contribute to social disruption. In other words, once irreversible, environmental degradation becomes an independent variable.

Skeptics often use a different argument. They state that conflict arising from resource scarcity is not particularly interesting, because it has been common throughout human history. We maintain, though, that renewable-resource scarcities of the next 50 years will probably occur with a speed, complexity and magnitude unprecedented in history. Entire countries can now be deforested in a few decades, most of a region's topsoil can disappear in a generation, and acute ozone depletion may take place in as few as 20 years.

Unlike nonrenewable resources—including fossil fuels and iron ore—renewable resources are linked in highly complex, interdependent systems with many nonlinear and feedback relations. The overextraction of one resource can lead to multiple, unanticipated environmental problems and sudden scarcities when the system passes critical thresholds.

Our research suggests that the social and political turbulence set in motion by changing environmental conditions will not follow the commonly perceived pattern of scarcity conflicts. There are many examples in the past of one group or nation trying to seize the resources of another. For instance, during World War II, Japan sought to secure oil, minerals and other resources in China and Southeast Asia.

Currently, however, many threatened renewable resources are held in common—including the atmosphere and the oceans—which makes them unlikely to be the object of straightforward clashes. In addition, we have come to understand that scarcities of renewable resources often produce insidious and cumulative social effects, such as population displacement and economic disruption. These events can, in turn, lead to clashes between ethnic groups as well as to civil strife and insurgency. Although such conflicts may not be as conspicuous or dramatic as wars over scarce resources, they may have serious repercussions for the security interests of the developed and the developing worlds.

Human actions bring about scarcities of renewable resources in three principal ways. First, people can reduce the quantity or degrade the quality of these resources faster than they are renewed. This phenomenon is often referred to as the consumption of the resource's "capital": the capital generates "income" that can be tapped for human consumption. A sustainable economy can therefore be defined as one that leaves the capital intact and undamaged so that future generations can enjoy undiminished income. Thus, if topsoil creation in a region of farmland is 0.25 millimeter per year, then average soil loss should not exceed that amount.

The second source of scarcity is population growth. Over time, for instance, a given flow of water might have to be divided among a greater number of people. The final cause is change in the distribution of a resource within a society. Such a shift can concentrate supply in the hands of a few, subjecting the rest to extreme scarcity.

These three origins of scarcity can operate singly or in combination. In some cases, population growth by itself will set in motion social stress. Bangladesh, for example, does not suffer from debilitating soil degradation or from the erosion of agricultural land: the annual flooding of the Ganges and Brahmaputra rivers deposits a layer of silt that helps to maintain the fertility of the country's vast floodplains.

But the United Nations predicts that Bangladesh's current population of 120 million will reach 235 million by the year 2025. At about 0.08 hectare per capita, cropland is already desperately scarce. Population density is 785 people per square kilometer (in comparison, population density in the adjacent Indian state of Assam is 284 people per square kilometer). Because all the country's good agricultural land has been exploited, population growth will cut in half the amount of cropland available per capita by 2025. Flooding and inadequate national and community institutions for water control exacerbate the lack of land and the brutal poverty and turmoil it engenders.

Over the past 40 years, millions of people have migrated from Bangladesh to neighboring areas of India, where the standard of living is often better. Detailed data on the movements are few: the Bangladeshi government is reluctant to admit there is significant migration because the issue has become a major source of friction with India. Nevertheless, one of our researchers, Sanjoy Hazarika, an investigative journalist and reporter at the *New York Times* in New Delhi, pieced together demographic information and experts' estimates. He concludes that Bangladeshi migrants and their descendants have expanded the population of neighboring areas of India by 15 million. (Only one to two million of those people can be attributed to migrations during the 1971 war between India and Pakistan that resulted in the creation of Bangladesh.)

Three Views of the Role That Scarcity of Renewable Resources Plays in Violent Conflict

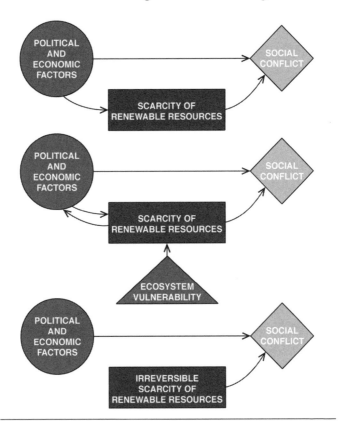

This enormous flux has produced pervasive social changes in the receiving Indian states. Conflict has been triggered by altered land distribution as well as by shifts in the balance of political and economic power between religious and ethnic groups. For instance, members of the Lalung tribe in Assam have long resented Bengali Muslim migrants: they accuse them of stealing the area's richest farmland. In early 1983, during a bitterly contested election for federal offices in the state, violence finally erupted. In the village of Nellie, Lalung tribespeople massacred nearly 1,700 Bengalis in one five-hour rampage.

In the state of Tripura the original Buddhist and Christian inhabitants now make up less than 30 percent of the population. The remaining percentage consists of Hindu migrants from either East Pakistan or Bangladesh. This shift in the ethnic balance precipitated a violent insurgency between 1980 and 1988 that was called off only after the government agreed to return land to dispossessed Tripuris and to stop the influx of Bangladeshis. As the migration has continued, however, this agreement is in jeopardy.

Population movements in this part of South Asia are, of course, hardly new. During the colonial period, the British imported Hindus from Calcutta to administer Assam, and Bengali was made the official language. As a result, the Assamese are particularly sensitive to the loss of political and cultural control in the state. And Indian politicians have often encouraged immigration in order to garner votes. Yet today changes in population density in Bangladesh are clearly contributing to the exodus. Although the contextual factors of religion and politics are important, they do not obscure the fact that a dearth of land in Bangladesh has been a force behind conflict.

In other parts of the world the three sources of scarcity interact to produce discord. Population growth and reductions in the quality and quantity of renewable resources can lead to large-scale development projects that can alter access to resources. Such a shift may lead to decreased supplies for poorer groups whose claims are violently opposed by powerful elites. A dispute that began in 1989 between Mauritanians and Senegalese in the Senegal River valley, which demarcates the common border between these countries, provides an example of such causality.

Senegal has fairly abundant agricultural land, but much of it suffers from severe wind erosion, loss of nutrients, salinization because of overirrigation and soil compaction caused by the intensification of agriculture. The country has an overall population density of 380 people per square kilometer and a population growth rate of 2.7 percent; in 25 years the population may double. In contrast, except for the Senegal River valley along its southern border and a few oases, Mauritania is for the most part arid desert and semiarid grassland. Its population density is very low, about 20 people per square kilometer, and the growth rate is 2.8 percent a year. The U.N. Food and Agriculture Organization has included both Mauritania and Senegal in its list of countries whose croplands cannot support current or projected populations without a large increase in agricultural inputs, such as fertilizer and irrigation.

Normally, the broad floodplains fringing the Senegal River support productive farming, herding and fishing based on the river's annual floods. During the 1970s, however, the prospect of chronic food shortages and a serious drought encouraged the region's governments to seek international financing for the Manantali Dam on the Bafing River tributary in Mali and for the Diama salt-intrusion barrage near the mouth of the Senegal River between Senegal and Mauritania. The dams were designed to regulate the river's flow for hydropower, to expand irrigated agriculture and to raise water levels in the dry season, permitting year-round barge transport from the Atlantic Ocean to land-locked Mali, which lies to the east of Senegal and Mauritania.

But the plan had unfortunate and unforeseen consequences. As anthropologist Michael M. Horowitz of the State University of New York at Binghamton has

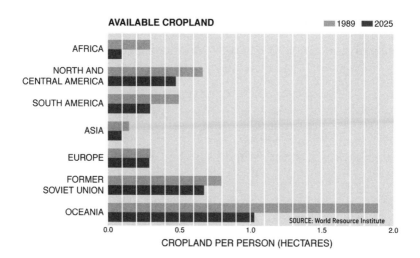

Available cropland is expected to decline in many parts of the world by 2025 as a result of population growth and the degradation of fertile land.

shown, anticipation of the new dams raised land values along the river in areas where high-intensity agriculture was to become feasible. The elite in Mauritania, which consists primarily of white Moors, then rewrote legislation governing land ownership, effectively abrogating the rights of black Africans to continue farming, herding and fishing along the Mauritanian riverbank.

There has been a long history of racism by white Moors in Mauritania toward their non-Arab, black compatriots. In the spring of 1989 the killing of Senegalese farmers by Mauritanians in the river basin triggered explosions of ethnic violence in the two countries. In Senegal almost all of the 17,000 shops owned by Moors were destroyed, and their owners were deported to Mauritania. In both countries several hundred people were killed, and the two nations nearly came to war. The Mauritanian regime used this occasion to activate the new land legislation, declaring the black Mauritanians who lived alongside the river to be "Senegalese," thereby stripping them of their citizenship; their property was seized. Some 70,000 of the black Mauritanians were forcibly expelled to Senegal, from where some launched raids to retrieve expropriated cattle. Diplomatic relations between the two countries have now been restored, but neither has agreed to allow the expelled population to return or to compensate them for their losses.

We see a somewhat different causal process in many parts of the world: unequal access to resources combines with population growth to produce environmental damage. This phenomenon can contribute to economic deprivation that spurs insurgency and rebellion. In the Philippines, Spanish and American colonial policies left behind a grossly inequitable distribution of land. Since the 1960s, the introduction of green revolution technologies has permitted a dramatic increase in lowland production of grain for domestic consumption and of cash crops that has helped pay the country's massive external debt.

This modernization has raised demand for agricultural labor. Unfortunately, though, the gain has been overwhelmed by a population growth rate of 2.5 to 3.0 percent. Combined with the maldistribution of good cropland and an economic crisis in the first half of the 1980s, this growth produced a surge in agricultural unemployment.

With insufficient rural or urban industrialization to absorb excess labor, there has been unrelenting downward pressure on wages. Economically desperate, millions of poor agricultural laborers and landless peasants have migrated to shantytowns in already overburdened cities, such as Manila; millions of others have moved to the least productive—and often most ecologically vulnerable—territories, such as steep hillsides.

In these uplands, settlers use fire to clear forested or previously logged land. They bring with them little ability to protect the fragile ecosystem. Their small-scale logging, charcoal production and slash-and-burn farming often cause erosion, landslides and changes in hydrologic patterns. This behavior has initiated a cycle of falling food production, the clearing of new plots and further land degradation. Even marginally fertile land is becoming hard to find in many places, and economic conditions are critical for peasants.

The country has suffered from serious internal strife for many decades. But two researchers, Celso R. Roque, the former undersecretary of the environment of the Philippines, and his colleague Maria I. Garcia, conclude that resource scarcity appears to be an increasingly powerful force behind the current communist-led insurgency. The upland struggle—including guerrilla attacks and assaults on military stations—is motivated by the economic deprivation of the landless agricultural laborers and poor farmers displaced into the hills, areas that are largely beyond the control of the central government. During the 1970s and 1980s, the New People's Army and the National Democratic Front found upland peasants receptive to revolutionary ideology, especially where coercive landlords and local governments left them little choice but to rebel or starve. The revolutionaries have built on indigenous beliefs and social structures to help the peasants focus their discontent.

Causal processes similar to those in the Philippines can be seen in many other regions around the planet, including the Himalayas, the Sahel, Indonesia, Brazil and Costa Rica. Population growth and unequal access to good land force huge numbers of people into cities or onto marginal lands. In the latter case, they cause environmental damage and become chronically poor. Eventually these people may be the source of persistent upheaval, or they may migrate yet again, stimulating ethnic conflicts or urban unrest elsewhere.

The short but devastating "Soccer War" in 1969 between El Salvador and Honduras involved just such a combination of factors. As William H. Durham of Stanford University has shown, changes in agriculture and land distribution beginning in the mid-19th century concentrated poor farmers in El Salvador's uplands. Although these peasants developed some understanding of land conservation, their growing numbers on very steep hillsides caused deforestation and erosion. A natural population growth rate of 3.5 percent further reduced land availability, and as a result many people moved to neighboring Honduras. Their eventual expulsion from Honduras precipitated a war in which several thousand people were killed in a few days. Durham notes that the competition for land in El Salvador leading to this conflict was not addressed in the war's aftermath and that it powerfully contributed to the country's subsequent, decade-long civil war.

In South Africa the white regime's past apartheid policies concentrated millions of blacks in the country's least productive and most ecologically sensitive territories. High natural birth rates exacerbated population densities. In 1980 rural areas of the Ciskei homeland supported 82 persons per square kilometer, whereas the surrounding Cape Province had a rural density of two. Homeland residents had, and have, little capital and few skills to manage resources. They remain the victims of corrupt and abusive local governments.

Sustainable development in such a situation is impossible. Wide areas have been completely stripped of trees for fuelwood, grazed down to bare dirt and eroded of topsoil. A 1980 report concluded that nearly 50 percent of Ciskei's land was moderately or severely eroded; close to 40 percent of its pasture was overgrazed. This loss of resources, combined with the lack of alternative employment and the social trauma caused by apartheid, has created a subsistence crisis in the homelands. Thousands of people have migrated to South African cities. The result is the rapid growth of squatter settlements and illegal townships that are rife with discord and that threaten the country's move toward democratic stability.

Dwindling natural resources can weaken the administrative capacity and authority of government, which may create opportunities for violent challenges to the state by political and military opponents. By contributing to rural poverty and rural-urban migration, scarcity of renewable resources expands the number of people needing assistance from the government. In response to growing city populations, states often introduce subsidies that distort prices and cause misallocations of capital, hindering economic productivity.

Simultaneously, the loss of renewable resources can reduce the production of wealth, thereby constraining tax revenues. For some countries, this widening gap between demands on the state and its capabilities may aggravate popular grievances, erode the state's legitimacy and escalate competition between elite factions as they struggle to protect their prerogatives.

Logging for export markets, as in Southeast Asia and West Africa, produces short-term economic gain for parts of the elite and may alleviate external debt. But it also jeopardizes long-term productivity. Forest removal decreases the land's ability to retain water during rainy periods. Flash floods then damage roads, bridges, irrigation systems and other valuable infrastructure. Erosion of hillsides silts up rivers, reducing their navigability and their capacity to generate hydroelectric power. Deforestation can also hinder crop production by altering regional hydrologic cycles and by plugging reservoirs and irrigation channels with silt.

In looking at China, Václav Smil of the University of Manitoba has estimated the combined effect of environmental problems on productivity. The main economic burdens he identifies are reduced crop yields caused by water, soil and air pollution; higher human morbidity resulting from air pollution; farmland loss because of construction and erosion; nutrient loss and flooding caused by erosion and deforestation; and timber loss arising from poor harvesting practices. Smil calculates the current annual cost to be at least 15 percent of China's gross domestic product; he is convinced the toll will rise steeply in the coming decades. Smil also estimates that tens of millions of Chinese will try to leave the country's impoverished interior and northern regions—where water and fuelwood are desperately scarce and the land often badly damaged—for the booming coastal cities. He anticipates bitter disputes among these regions over water sharing and migration. Taken together, these economic and political stresses may greatly weaken the Chinese state.

Water shortages in the Middle East will become worse in the future and may also contribute to political discord. Although figures vary, Miriam R. Lowi of Princeton University estimates that the average amount of renewable fresh water available annually to Israel is about 1,950 million cubic meters (mcm). Sixty percent comes from groundwater, the rest from river flow, floodwater and wastewater recycling. Current Israeli demand—including that of settlements in the occupied territories and the Golan Heights—is about 2,200 mcm. The annual deficit of about 200 mcm is met by over-pumping aquifers.

As a result, the water table in some parts of Israel and the West Bank has been dropping significantly. This depletion can cause the salinization of wells and the infiltration of seawater from the Mediterranean. At the same time, Israel's population is expected to increase from the present 4.6 million to 6.5 million people in the year 2020, an estimate that does not include immigration from the former Soviet Union.

Available Water

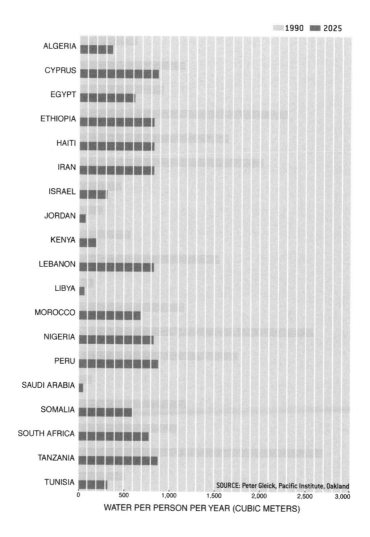

1990   2025

SOURCE: Peter Gleick, Pacific Institute, Oakland

WATER PER PERSON PER YEAR (CUBIC METERS)

Water shortages may be severe in the future. In 2025 several nations will have less than 1,000 cubic meters of water per person—the minimum amount considered necessary for an industrialized nation.

191

Based on this projected expansion, the country's water demand could exceed 2,600 mcm by 2020.

Two of the three main aquifers on which Israel depends lie for the most part under the West Bank, although their waters drain into Israel. Thus, nearly 40 percent of the groundwater Israel uses originates in occupied territory. To protect this important source, the Israeli government has strictly limited water use on the West Bank. Of the 650 mcm of all forms of water annually available there, Arabs are allowed to use only 125 mcm. Israel restricts the number of wells Arabs can drill in the territory, the amount of water Arabs are allowed to pump and the times at which they can draw irrigation water.

The differential in water access on the West Bank is marked: on a per capita basis, Jewish settlers consume about four times as much water as Arabs. Arabs are not permitted to drill new wells for agricultural purposes, although Mekorot (the Israeli water company) has drilled more than 30 for settlers. Arab agriculture in the region has suffered because some Arab wells have become saline as a result of deeper Israeli wells drilled nearby. The Israeli water policy, combined with the confiscation of agricultural land for settlers as well as other Israeli restrictions on Palestinian agriculture, has encouraged many West Bank Arabs to abandon farming. Those who have done so have become either unemployed or day laborers within Israel.

The entire Middle East faces increasingly grave and tangled problems of water scarcity, and many experts believe these will affect the region's stability. Concerns over water access contributed to tensions preceding the 1967 Arab-Israeli War; the war gave Israel control over most of the Jordan Basin's water resources. The current Middle East peace talks include multilateral meetings on water rights, motivated by concerns about impending scarcities.

Although "water wars" are possible in the future, they seem unlikely given the preponderance of Israeli military power. More probably, in the context of historical ethnic and political disputes, water shortages will aggravate tensions and unrest within societies in the Jordan River basin. In recent U.S. congressional testimony, Thomas Naff of the University of Pennsylvania noted that "rather than warfare among riparians in the immediate future. . . what is more likely to ensue from water-related crises in this decade is internal civil disorder, changes in regimes, political radicalization and instability."

Scarcities of renewable resources clearly can contribute to conflict, and the frequency of such unrest will probably grow in the future. Yet some analysts maintain that scarcities are not important in and of themselves. What is important, they contend, is whether people are harmed by them. Human suffering might be avoided if political and economic systems provide the incentives

Urbanization in Less Developed Regions

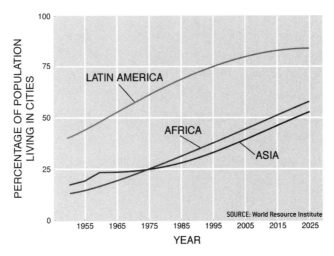

Growth of cities, in part a result of increasing rural poverty and of migration, will be dramatic in the developing world.

and wherewithal that enable people to alleviate the harmful effects of environmental problems.

Our research has not produced firm evidence for or against this argument. We need to know more about the variables that affect the supply of human ingenuity in response to environmental change. Technical ingenuity is needed for the development of, for example, new agricultural and forestry technologies that compensate for environmental deterioration. Social ingenuity is needed for the creation of institutions that buffer people from the effects of degradation and provide the right incentives for technological innovation.

The role of social ingenuity as a precursor to technical ingenuity is often overlooked. An intricate and stable system of markets, legal regimes, financial agencies and educational and research institutions is a prerequisite for the development and distribution of many technologies—including new grains adapted to dry climates and eroded soils, alternative cooking technologies that compensate for the loss of firewood and water-conservation technologies. Not only are poor countries ill endowed with these social resources, but their ability to create and maintain them will be weakened by the very environmental woes such nations hope to address.

The evidence we have presented here suggests there are significant causal links between scarcities of renewable resources and violence. To prevent such turmoil, nations should put greater emphasis on reducing such scarcities. This means that rich and poor countries alike must cooperate to restrain population growth, to implement a more equitable distribution of wealth within and among their societies, and to provide for sustainable development.

The Authors

Thomas F. Homer-Dixon, Jeffrey H. Boutwell and George W. Rathjens are co-directors of the project on Environmental Change and Acute Conflict, which is jointly sponsored by the University of Toronto and the American Academy of Arts and Sciences. Homer-Dixon received his Ph.D. in political science from the Massachusetts Institute of Technology in 1989 and is now coordinator of the Peace and Conflict Studies Program at the University of Toronto. Boutwell, who also received his Ph.D. from M.I.T., is associate executive officer and program director of International Security Studies at the American Academy of Arts and Sciences. Rathjens earned his doctorate in chemistry at the University of California, Berkeley, and is currently professor of political science at M.I.T.

4 Possible Responses to Environmental Concerns

Sometimes, solutions to apparently unsolvable problems are staring us right in the face. The next article looks to nature for guidance in solving problems concerning garbage and other waste materials. The issue not only pertains to the environment but also affects the economy. Any time that businesses and consumers throw something out and it winds up in a landfill, the object and the materials used to make it go to waste. Can you imagine if nature operated in such a manner? Ecosystems would never survive.

In food webs, as author Robert Frosch describes, animals eat plants and other animals, and then they are consumed by other animals or microbes. Little if anything is wasted because the nutrients continually pass from one individual to another. Even when an animal eats a fruit and drops the peel to the ground, that discarded part will either be consumed by other organisms or decompose and then release its nutrients where it fell.

The challenge now is to apply nature's miraculous system to industrial processes.

Garbage collection services in recent years have improved so that, for example, soda cans and bottles may be recycled. However, more needs to be done to reduce waste from other materials. —JV

"The Industrial Ecology of the 21st Century"
by Robert A. Frosch
Scientific American, September 1995

The end of the 20th century has seen a subtle change in the way many industries are confronting environmental concerns: they are shifting away from the treatment or disposal of industrial waste and toward the elimination of its very creation. This strategy attempts to get ahead of the problem, so that society is not destined to face an ever growing mass of waste emanating from the end of a discharge pipe or the brim of a garbage pail. It seems likely that the next century will see an acceleration of this trend, a clear departure from the past emphasis—by industry, by government regulators and even by most environmental organizations—on late-stage cleanup.

The old attitude often resulted only in manufacturers dumping waste into their own "backyards," thus generating a good deal of what might be called industrial archaeology. That heritage currently puts many firms into the environmental cleanup business, whether they like it or not. But in the 21st century, industry may behave quite differently, so as to avoid creating more expensive burial sites that society will have to suffer or pay to clean up all over again.

What most people would like to see is a way to use industrial waste productively. Waste is, after all, *wasteful*. It is money going out the door in the form of processed material and its embodied energy. To avoid this inefficiency, manufacturers of the next century must consider how to design and produce products in such a way as to make the control of waste and pollution part of their enterprise, not just an afterthought. They will need to pay attention to the entire product life cycle, worrying not only about the materials used and created in the course of manufacturing but also about what happens to a product at the end of its life. Will it become a disposal problem, or can it become a source of refined material and energy?

Manufacturers are just beginning to seek new approaches in what may well become a comprehensive revolution. As such movements often do, these efforts are producing new ideas and a new set of buzzwords. Engineers had previously spoken of "design for manu- facturing" and "design for assembly," and now we have added "design for disassembly," "design for recycling" and "design for environment" to our vocabulary. These terms mean simply that from the very start we are paying attention to the potential effects of excess waste and pollution in manufacturing.

Overcoming these problems is in part a technological problem—clever new technologies that can reduce or recycle wastes will surely play a valuable role. But the answer will not depend entirely on inventing breakthrough technologies. Rather it may hinge on coordinating what are fairly conventional methods in more prudent ways and in developing legal and market structures that will allow suitable innovation. These efforts will involve complex considerations of product and process design, economics and optimization, as well as regulation and handling of hazardous materials. Strangely, there has been relatively little general examination of these issues, although there are many individual cases in which such thinking has been employed.

For example, Kumar Patel of AT&T Bell Laboratories has described an interesting approach being taken in a section of its microelectronics fabrication business. Engineers at that division of Bell Labs were concerned because several of the raw materials, such as gallium arsenide, were particularly nasty. They dealt with this difficulty by using, in effect, the military technology of binary chemical weapons, in which two chemicals that are not very hazardous individually combine within a weapon to make one tremendously hazardous substance. Bell Labs now avoids having to keep an inventory of one highly toxic material through a simple process that brings together its much less hazardous chemical constituents right at the spot where the combined compound is used. This is essentially a just-in-time delivery system that matches production to need and obviates disposal of excess. Bell Labs concluded that the company amortized the investment in new equipment in less than a year by eliminating the extra costs of storing, transporting and occasionally disposing of the hazardous compound.

A Lesson from Nature

Beyond solving as much of the waste problem as possible within each company, we have to think about industry in the future on a larger scale. We need to examine how the total industrial economy generates waste and pollutants that might damage the environment. Viewing industry as an interwoven system of production and consumption, one finds that the natural world can teach us quite a bit. The analog with nature suggests the name "industrial ecology" for this idea (although this term is increasingly coming into use for a diverse set of practices that might make industry pollute less).

The natural ecological system, as an integrated whole, minimizes waste. Nothing, or almost nothing, that is produced by one organism as waste is not for another organism a source of usable material and energy. Dead or alive, all plants and animals and their wastes are food for something. Microbes consume and decompose waste, and these microorganisms in turn are eaten by other creatures in the food web. In this marvelous natural system, matter and energy go around and around in large cycles, passing through a series of interacting organisms.

With this insight from the natural ecological system, we are beginning to think about whether there are ways to connect different industrial processes that produce waste, particularly hazardous waste. A fully developed industrial ecology might not necessarily minimize the waste from any specific factory or industrial sector but should act to minimize the waste produced overall.

This is not really a new or startling idea. There are companies that have sought this minimization for a long time. The chemical and petrochemical industries are probably ahead of most others. They characteristically think in terms of turning as much as possible of what they process into useful product. But in the future, industrial countries will want all producers to be thinking about how they can alter manufacturing, products and materials so that the ensemble minimizes both waste and cost. Such requirements need not be onerous: a company might easily change to a more expensive manufacturing process if it prevents the generation of waste that the firm had to pay to have taken away and if it creates materials for which there are customers.

Many requirements must be met for this redirection to be accomplished. As incentive for designing and producing something specifically so that it can be reused, companies will need reliable markets. Many early attempts at recycling failed because they just collected materials—a pointless exercise unless somebody actually wants to use them. If there are going to be markets for what would otherwise be waste, information will need to be available on who has what, who needs what, who

continued on page 206

The Ultimate Incinerators

While the world waits for industry to develop processes so efficient they do not produce waste, the problem of safely disposing of our garbage persists. The idea of loading toxic or other forms of waste on board a space-craft and blasting them into the sun seems, at first glance, a nice solution to the earth's trash woes. At 5,500 degrees Celsius, the surface of Sol would leave little intact. But considering the amount of garbage each human produces—three to four pounds per day, on average—launches would simply be too expensive to conduct regularly. Add the possibility of a malfunction during liftoff, and space shots of waste seem impractical.

Instead some researchers are taking the opposite tack: bringing a bit of the sun to the earth. By sending a strong electric current through a rarefied gas, they can create plasma—an intensely hot gas in which electrons have been separated from atomic nuclei. The plasma, in turn, reaches up to 10,000 degrees C. (Conventional incinerators, using fossil fuels, reach no more than 2,000 degrees C.) In the presence of this demonic heat, hydrocarbons, PCBs and other toxins that lace contaminated soil and ash break down, yielding molten slag that hardens into inert and harmless glassy rocks suitable for road gravel. Unlike their smoke-belching conventional counterparts, plasma incinerators burn more cleanly, emitting one fifth as much gas. Some designers propose capturing this gas, which is combustible, for use as fuel.

continued on following page

continued from previous page

With so many pluses, it seems that plasma should have been cooking waste a long time ago. The hurdle has been economic: plasma can vaporize nonhazardous waste for about $65 a ton, whereas landfilling costs less than half that amount. But as landfill space dwindles and stricter environmental codes are adopted, plasma waste destruction is becoming more competitive. For treatment of toxic waste, it may even be cheaper. Daniel R. Cohn of the Massachusetts Institute of Technology estimates that a full-scale plant could operate for less than $300 a ton—less than half the current cost of disposing of hazardous waste.

The more reasonable economics have encouraged many institutions to set up pilot furnaces. "The whole technology is starting to pick up around the world," notes Louis J. Circeo of the Georgia Institute of Technology, where some of the largest furnaces are located. Near Bordeaux, France, a plant destroys asbestos at the rate of 100 tons a week. The Japanese city of Matsuyama has a facility designed to handle the 300 tons of incinerator ash that comes from the daily burning of 3,000 tons of municipal waste. Construction of a furnace that could torch 12 tons of medical waste a day is under way at Kaiser Permanente's San Diego hospital. Circeo thinks it is even feasible to treat existing landfills: just lower some plasma torches down nearby boreholes.

Plasma need not be hot; it can also exist at room temperature. Cohn and his colleagues are testing the idea of using "cold" plasma to destroy toxic vapors. The physicists create such plasma by firing an electron beam into a gas, a process that severs electrons from nuclei and thus converts the gas into plasma. Volatile organic compounds passed through the plasma are attacked by the free electrons, which break down the chemicals. Last year the workers tested their trailer-size unit at the Department of Energy's Hanford Nuclear Reservation site in Richard, Wash., where up to two million pounds of industrial solvents have been dumped since the complex's founding during the Manhattan Project. They vacuumed out some of the carbon tetrachloride in the ground and then pumped it into the chamber of cold plasma, which transformed the toxin into less harmful products that were subsequently broken down into carbon dioxide, carbon monoxide, water and salt.

It may be a while before toxic waste is a distant memory or before you can zap your kitchen trash into nothingness with the flick of a switch, but many researchers are betting that plasma waste destruction is becoming a reality. Circeo, for instance, hopes to raise $10 million for a plasma plant that can destroy the 20 tons of garbage that revelers and others at the 1996 Olympic Games in Atlanta are expected to generate daily. "In five to 10 years," he predicts, "you're going to see plasma technology springing up all over the place."

—*The Editors of* Scientific American

continued from page 202

uses what. This information is typically inaccessible now because companies tend to be secretive about their waste streams. (If competitors know about the by-products produced, they might deduce protected trade secrets.) We will have to invent ways to get around this difficulty.

Antirecycling Laws

In addition to the need for more complete market information, society requires a novel kind of regulation to make a true industrial ecology possible. Frustrations with regulation frequently arise because we have fostered and developed environmental laws that attempt to deal with one problem at a time. The current regulatory framework focuses on disposing of or treating industrial wastes without regard for the possibility of minimizing or reusing them. In fact, it often acts to thwart recycling. Once a substance is classified as hazardous waste, it becomes extraordinarily difficult to do anything useful with it, even if the material is identical to a "virgin" industrial chemical readily bought and sold on the open market.

For example, if a manufacturer produces waste containing cyanide, a toxic hydrocarbon or a heavy metal, the company will likely be controlled by strict environmental laws. Unless the firm can overcome excruciatingly complex bureaucratic barriers, it will probably not be allowed to process that material into a salable product or even to transport it (except to a disposal site). Yet anyone can easily go to a chemical manufacturer and buy cyanide, hydrocarbon solvents or heavy metal compounds that have been newly produced. (Their manufacturer generally has a standing permit for packaging, transporting and selling these substances.)

A particularly interesting example comes from the automotive industry's treatment of steel. Anticorrosion measures produce a zinc-rich sludge that in the past was sent to a smelter to recover the zinc and put it back into the process stream. But a decade ago regulations began listing such wastewater treatment sludges as hazardous. The unintended consequence was that the smelters could no longer use the sludge, because it had become, in name, a hazardous material—the regulatory requirements for accepting it were too severe. The zinc-rich sludge was redirected to landfills, thereby increasing costs for automobile manufacturers and producing a waste disposal problem for the rest of society.

This situation clearly illustrated what can be a serious problem: well-meant environmental regulation can have the bizarre effect of increasing both the amount of waste created and the amount to be disposed, because it puts up high barriers to reuse. It might be viewed as antirecycling regulation. This peculiarity appears to have occurred essentially by inadvertence: industrial supplies, whether toxic or not, are controlled by different statutes—and often by a different part of the government—than are materials considered waste. A priority for the future will be a cleanup of that aspect of the nation's regulatory machinery.

With adequate effort the next century will see many improvements in environmental laws as well as in specific environmental technologies. But the most important advance of all may be the fundamental reorganization that allows used materials to flow freely between consumers and manufacturers, between one firm and the next and between one industry and another. As much as we need to excavate the industrial archaeology left over from the past, we also need to draw lessons for the future from these ghastly sites, create an industrial ecological vision and formulate a system of law and practice to enable it.

The Author

Robert A. Frosch has served as assistant executive director of the United Nations Environment Program and as administrator of the National Aeronautics and Space Administration. In 1993 he retired as vice president of General Motors Corporation, where he was in charge of the North American Operations Research and Development Center. He is now a senior research fellow at the John F. Kennedy School of Government at Harvard University.

Ideas on paper do not always produce their intended results, as this next article demonstrates. It seemed like a good idea when, a few decades ago, conservationists wanted consumers to purchase goods originating in endangered areas, such as nuts grown in tropical rain forests. Producers negotiated deals with farmers and other suppliers, hoping that the money earned would prevent more destructive uses of the rain forests and other properties. According to authors Jared Hardner and Richard Rice, this practice of so-called sustainable agriculture is not enough to prevent deforestation and its effects, such as habitat loss for endangered plants and animals.

Instead, Hardner and Rice propose that efforts should be directed toward what they refer to as conservation concessions. Rather than just negotiating deals pertaining to the agricultural goods, the concessions involve outright leasing of the lands in question. Conservationists can then prevent destructive practices from occurring on the land, but control remains in the hands of the people who live on or near the land. —JV

"Rethinking Green Consumerism"
by Jared Hardner and Richard Rice
Scientific American, May 2002

Over the past decade, one popular tropical conservation effort has been to encourage consumers to pay more for products that are cultivated or harvested in ecologically sensitive ways. Myriad international development projects have promoted these so-called sustainable practices in forests and farms around the world. Ordinary citizens in the U.S. and Europe participate by choosing to buy timber, coffee and other agricultural goods that are certified as having met such special standards during production. One of the best known of these certified, or "green," products is shade-grown coffee beans, which are cultivated in the shady forest understory rather than in sunny fields where all the trees have been cut down.

Efforts to develop green products deserve support and praise. But in the context of the global economy, sustainable agriculture and consumer actions alone will not be enough to conserve the plants and animals that are most threatened by deforestation. We believe that a bold new approach, which we call conservation concessions, provides a potentially powerful way to expand the green market from its present dependence on products to the broader notion of green services—the opportunity to purchase biodiversity preservation directly.

The feasibility of this strategy relies on economics. Huge tracts of public forest in the developing world are being leased for less than $1 per hectare a year. At those prices, conservation organizations, which have long demonstrated a willingness to pay for the preservation of biodiversity, can afford to outbid competitors for land leases and to compensate local people to manage the intact ecosystems. These agreements are legally and economically no different from logging contracts or any other business deal that grants control over natural resources to a particular group. Indeed, the income that developing countries can generate in this way is equivalent to, and often more stable than, what they could earn through the volatile international markets for timber and agricultural goods.

No Other Choices

One of the greatest advantages of conservation concessions is that they dispel the notion that habitat destruction is inevitable if ecosystems are to generate financial benefits. During a study of cocoa economics in Ghana in the spring of 2000, an official in that country's department of forestry explained to one of our research partners, Eduard Niesten, that Ghana's government cannot be expected to set aside more than the 20 percent of its prized high-canopy forest zone that is already protected by national law. The rest must be used for economic progress, the official said. This pessimistic sentiment is widespread among governments and residents of many developing countries, where economic planning often includes rapid growth of the production of agricultural commodities, especially after logging operations have cleared the land. These activities represent an attractive—and perhaps the only—development option in tropical countries, which tend to have an abundance of land and unskilled labor but insufficient capital to finance more costly endeavors, such as industry.

To examine this issue more closely, we formed a research team with six other investigators at

Conservation International's Center for Applied Biodiversity Science in Washington, D.C. Our aim was to study agricultural commodities that are produced in areas designated by ecologists as the world's richest and most threatened in terms of biodiversity. These 25 so-called biodiversity hot spots, which encompass only 1.4 percent of the earth's land surface, have lost at least 70 percent of their primary vegetation. They are also prime habitats for 44 percent of all vascular plant species and 35 percent of all land-dwelling vertebrate species. Based on this three-year study, our team determined that in addition to logging for timber, natural-habitat destruction is rapid and extensive to accommodate the production of five agricultural commodities: beef, soybeans, palm oil, coffee and cocoa.

In the 1980s the expansion of cattle ranches in South America was widely publicized. This activity accounted for 44 percent of deforestation on the continent during that decade. Today one of the greatest threats to South America's tropical biodiversity is the expanding production of soybeans, most of which goes to feed livestock. Since the 1970s soybean cultivation has grown by 13 million hectares in Brazil alone—the fastest expansion of any agricultural product in the tropics known to date. Government subsidies have allowed this activity to move into areas never before touched by agriculture. In neighboring Bolivia, the area devoted to this crop has grown by an average of nearly 35 percent a year since the mid-1960s and is fast approaching one million hectares.

Elsewhere natural forests are being converted at an alarming rate to cultivation of the other three crops in our study. Spread ubiquitously around the world's biodiversity hot spots are coffee and cocoa, occupying 11 and eight million hectares, respectively. Their cultivation has replaced as much as 80 percent of Ivory Coast's original forests. Malaysia leads the production of palm oil, cultivating three million hectares out of the total six million devoted to this commodity globally. Indonesia, which currently grows oil palm on 2.5 million hectares, has vowed to overtake its neighbor as the world's leading producer by planting the 15 million additional hectares that the government has already slated for oil palm plantations.

Certainly the intention of people who convert biologically diverse ecosystems to agriculture or logged forests is to improve their economic lot in life. The sad irony is that these prospects are often unreliable. When countries choose logging and agriculture for lack of better economic options, they often are not competitive in global markets. Indeed, the very nature of export commodity markets is that many producers are not profitable for years at a time because of chronic oversupply. The annual harvest of cocoa and accumulated stocks, for example, exceeded consumption by between 30 and 70 percent each year from 1971 to 1999. Cultivators in West Africa recently resorted to burning their crops in a desperate protest of the situation. Another striking example played out in Bolivia, where in 1996 the imposition of a new tax of $1 per hectare on

The Limits of Buying Green

A popular strategy for slowing the destruction of tropical forests has been to promote ecologically friendly practices within the agriculture and logging industries. But demand for coffee, timber and other "green" goods that are produced according to these certified practices originates almost entirely in Europe and the U.S., where consumers are willing to pay premium prices to support conservation. These niche markets play an important role in conservation efforts, but they have serious limits.

Unreliable profits restrict the markets for coffee and cocoa. Whether or not they produce green goods, all cultivators of these products must face the uncoordinated nature of global production, which often results in vast oversupply. Cocoa production swelled throughout the 1980s and 1990s, for instance, despite a punishing decline in price. For green consumerism to work in this context, conservationists must find ways not only to make cultivation and harvesting ecologically sound but also to ensure that the products will be profitable in a competitive global market.

A different problem confines the market for green timber. Organizations such as the Mexico-based nonprofit Forest Stewardship Council have certified more than five million hectares of logging activity in Asia, Africa and Latin America. The problem is that almost all the green timber produced in these forests is sold in Europe and the U.S., which together import less than 6.5 percent of the 228 million cubic meters of all timber—green or otherwise—that is produced in the tropics every year. The vast majority of uncertified logging serves the economies outside these regions.

The worse-case scenario occurs when uncertified logging occurs in biodiversity hot spots such as Madagascar, where most of the timber harvested will become charcoal that local people burn for fuel. This island country, which is less than 2 percent the size of neighboring Africa, harbors a staggering diversity of living things that are found nowhere else on the planet, including at least 8,000 species of flowering plant. Madagascar shelters 12 percent of all living primate species, 36 percent of all primate families, and 33 species of lemur that exist virtually nowhere else, making it possibly the world's single most important area for conservation of these animals. And yet because the trees are consumed domestically, wealthy foreign consumers looking to "buy green" have no opportunity to influence the logging of these priceless forest habitats.   —J. H. and R. R.

the country's 22 million hectares of timber concessions resulted in nearly 17 million hectares being abandoned by loggers. In other words, the potential net returns for logging these forests were so low that an additional cost of $1 per hectare per year was enough to make most companies avoid these investments.

No matter the level of economic payoff, all these situations can portend widespread, irreversible loss of biodiversity. The concept of sustainable forestry and farming practices was born of this dilemma—the need to promote economic development while mitigating its probable course of ecological destruction. But our recent studies have convinced us that attempting to give green consumers broader access to agricultural markets is not necessarily a winning option for economic development or conservation in many settings. The share of the global agricultural market that is occupied by green goods is largely limited to those consumers in Europe and the U.S. who have the money for, and an interest in, purchasing such products. This reality effectively eliminates the potential for curtailing deforestation related to many agricultural products— for example, soybeans from Brazil that are eaten by livestock, oil palm in Indonesia that is cultivated for domestic consumption, and trees in Madagascar that are burned locally as fuel [*see box on page 214*].

Even when certified goods—such as coffee, timber and beef—do reach wealthy consumers, the effect is not as significant as some may think. Less than 1 percent of the coffee imported into the U.S. is certified for social or ecological reasons. What is more, most of the land newly devoted to growing coffee beans is for robusta, usually sold in developing countries as instant coffee, rather than arabica, the product sold most commonly in cafes of the industrial world. Green timber fares no better. Even if every board foot of wood imported into the U.S. and Europe from tropical countries were certified, it would make up only 6.5 percent of total production from the tropics. The rest is being sold in regions where consumers have little or no interest in certified timber. Similarly, organically produced beef is growing in popularity in industrial countries. But international trade in beef represents only between 1 and 3 percent of global production; in the developing world, beef production is growing at more than 3 percent a year, primarily to serve domestic markets.

Marketing Green Services

The more we studied the conservation impacts of timber and agricultural commodity markets, the more convinced we became that attempting to support these markets through price premiums for green products is not the only way to encourage conservation. This situation seemed especially tragic when we considered the high demand for biodiversity protection among the international community. A common misperception is that conservation cannot compete directly with most other economic uses of natural resources; in reality, the conservation economy is quite large. The international community—including governments, multilateral development banks and conservation groups—spends at least half a billion dollars annually on biodiversity conservation in the tropics.

This figure is only a small fraction of the global budget that could be directed to biodiversity-rich countries if better investment mechanisms existed.

In 1999 an example from Bolivia showed us just how far these financial resources can go. That year Conservation International paid a logging company $100,000 to retire its 45,000-hectare timber concession. As part of the deal, the Bolivian government agreed to integrate the area into adjacent Madidi National Park. Bottom line: an area three times the size of Washington, D.C., received permanent protection for less than the average price of a house in that city.

Working with timber concessions or other lease arrangements enables conservationists to avoid the problems associated with purchasing land outright. Some governments balk at the idea of foreign investors taking permanent control of parts of their territories, especially if they are trying to ensure a renewable stream of revenue from their natural resources. For the same reasons, incorporating land into national parks—as conservationists were able to convince the Bolivian government to do—is also a rare opportunity. That is why the Bolivia experience, and others like it, inspired us to take advantage of the low prices for which millions of hectares of forest could be leased in the tropics.

We developed the conservation concession approach to leasing land with several major goals in mind [see box on page 220]. Most important, perhaps, was that a portion of the concession payments would be directed to local communities to support employment and social services. In the same way that a logging company would pay local residents wages and benefits to work in the mills, the financier of the conservation concession would hire them to preserve the forest.

Once we had developed a clear set of criteria for this newfangled green services market, we set off to create a series of pilot conservation concessions. Among the first countries we visited, early in 2000, was Peru. There we planned to compete for part of the 800,000 hectares of Amazon forest that the government was putting up for lease in an international auction. What transpired during our negotiations confirmed our theory that the economic value of forest resources in Peru—and many other regions of the world—is poor at best. Indeed, the auction began with a proposed minimum bid of between $1 and $4 per hectare a year and involved forestry companies from Europe and North and South America in addition to us. In a matter of months, however, the auction was called off because the other potential bidders lost interest in these concessions, presumably because the base price was too high. The fate of that particular forest remains to be determined, but we had planted a seed that took root in the fertile ground prepared by the Peruvian conservation community.

Peru had been undergoing the final revisions of its forest and wildlife law, a process in which several conservation groups were seeking alternatives to logging leases for Peru's forests. In April 2001 the government chose to include conservation concessions as a legal use of its 67 million hectares of public forest. We had entered the original bidding arena without knowing for

A New Green Market

Land set aside for conservation is often deemed an economic asset gone to waste. A new market for green services promises to eliminate this trade-off. International willingness to pay for conservation reflects growing demand for protection of the world's biodiversity, which many developing countries can readily supply. The logic behind this new market is simple: landowners lease natural resources to conservationists, who pay the same as or more than logging companies or other destructive users. These so-called conservation concessions not only protect the land but also finance conservation services and provide employment for local people. A properly executed conservation concession:

ENABLES HOST COUNTRIES TO CAPITALIZE ON THEIR AMPLE SUPPLY OF BIODIVERSITY-RICH HABITATS. The concession approach alleviates economic reliance on volatile timber and agricultural commodity markets and allows tropical countries to benefit economically by protecting their natural resources. This benefit can be achieved without depreciating the value of the natural resource and without damaging wildlife habitats or other aspects of the environment.

STIMULATES ECONOMIC DEVELOPMENT BY MIMICKING THE PAYMENT STRUCTURE OF OTHER BUSINESS TRANSACTIONS. Payments cover government taxes and fees, lost employment, and capital investment and are made in hard currency. Part of these fees is directed to the local communities to create jobs and invest in social programs.

OFFERS IMMEDIATE, TRANSPARENT PROTECTION FOR THE LAND IN QUESTION. The tangible nature of conservation concessions offers a clear way to quantify the payoff of biodiversity investments. They should also appeal to corporations seeking methods to offset the environmental impacts of their operations with unambiguous benefits.

CATALYZES CONSERVATION IN SITUATIONS WHERE CREATING A NATIONAL PARK MAY BE INFEASIBLE. Conservation concessions provide governments with an economically sound motive for creating protected areas that extend beyond park systems. Concession payments also ensure long-term management of these areas, in contrast to many underfunded national parks.

REDUCES RISK OF FAILURE BY ESTABLISHING ONGOING ECONOMIC INCENTIVE FOR COOPERATION. Substantial financial risk accompanies business investments in many developing countries, but a well-constructed incentive system based on annual payments in return for resource monitoring and other conservation services should dramatically reduce the temptation to break a concession agreement. —*J. H. and R. R.*

certain that we would be allowed to compete, so this was good news. At around that time, a Peruvian conservation group, the Amazon Conservation Association, approached us. The group's members wanted to use a conservation concession to secure critical natural habitat where they were setting up an ecological research station. Under the new Peruvian law, concessions could be acquired by applying for specific areas of interest to the bidder. We leaped at the chance to help launch Peru's first conservation concession.

Thanks to the scientific and community work of the Amazon Conservation Association, legal advice from the Peruvian Environmental Law Society (SPDA), assistance from independent environmental consultant Enrique Toledo, and the enthusiastic support of Peru's Minister of Agriculture, Carlos Amat y Leon, Peru established the Los Amigos conservation concession in July 2001. The agreement centered on a renewable 40-year lease for the conservation management and study of 130,000 hectares of tropical forest. This land forms part of an ecological corridor that links Manu and Bahuaja-Sonene national parks in Peru and protects many of that country's 25,000 species of flora and 1,700 species of birds.

Catching On

Over the course of our Los Amigos negotiations, we also conducted discussions for pilot projects in Guyana and Guatemala. In September 2000 the government of Guyana issued to Conservation International an exploratory permit for a conservation concession of approximately 80,000 hectares in the southern part of the country. During the subsequent months, we have worked with forest commission officials to negotiate the terms of a renewable 25-year contract. We hope to conclude the deal for this uninhabited area of forest later this year.

In Guatemala the national government had already issued timber concessions within the country's two-million-hectare Maya Biosphere Reserve to local communities. These people, who live within the reserve's multiple-use zone, where logging and other economic activities are permitted, are currently producing certified green timber from their forests. Two communities, however, have proposed to forgo logging and instead lease standing trees—and the obligation to protect the ecosystem in which they reside—to conservationists. The communities, together representing about 110 households, could use their new revenue stream from the proposed concession deal to pay salaries for conservation managers, to invest in projects such as guiding tourists to nearby archaeological sites, and to provide community social services such as education and health care. The proposed concessions, which would preserve both pristine forest and a wealth of Mayan ruins, span approximately 75,000 hectares bordering a national park [*see box on page 224*]. The Guatemala and Guyana deals, both developed and financed by Conservation International's Center for Applied Biodiversity Science and the Global

Partnering with Parks

National parks are an important component of any nation's conservation plan. In countries such as Guatemala and Indonesia, conservation concessions can extend the protection that parks offer, especially in areas that allow economic activities such as logging.

Guatemala

CONSERVATION CONTEXT: In 1990 the government of Guatemala created the two-million-hectare Maya Biosphere Reserve (MBR). The reserve includes a multiple-use area where commercial exploitation of forest resources is allowed, but its core zones are protected against all activities other than those judged to be environmentally benign, such as scientific research and ecotourism.

WHAT'S AT STAKE: The MBR is the largest remaining tropical forest in Guatemala, and it constitutes a major part of a Mesoamerican biological corridor that shelters the jaguar and other species with extensive ranges.

THE THREAT: Commercial logging (especially for mahogany) and agricultural invasion threaten forests in the multiple-use zone.

PROPOSED CONCESSION: Later this year Conservation International and its Guatemalan partner, ProPetén, hope to finalize conservation concession contracts with the communities that manage some 75,000 hectares of forest within the multiple-use zone. These additional conservation areas will begin to provide habitat links between the reserve's core zones of Tikal and El Mirador national parks.

Indonesia

CONSERVATION CONTEXT: Siberut National Park protects just under half of the 400,000-hectare island of Siberut, off the western coast of Sumatra. Only about 60 percent of the 205,000 hectares outside the park remain naturally forested.

WHAT'S AT STAKE: Three distinct types of forest habitat, including lowland tropical rain forest and freshwater swamp, support a diversity of life. Four of the island's primate species—Kloss gibbon, pig-tailed langur, Mentawai langur and Mentawai macaque—live nowhere else in the world. About 35,000 Mentawaian people, who maintain a Neolithic social structure, also rely heavily on the island's forest resources for their subsistence.

THE THREAT: Pending concessions for commercial logging and oil palm plantations threaten 80 percent of the island—including areas within the park.

PROPOSED CONCESSION: The local government of Siberut and Conservation International are negotiating a conservation concession that could extend the area protected by the park and curtail encroachment by logging and agriculture. —*J. H. and R. R.*

Conservation Fund, represent two very different settings for concessions.

At many turns in our negotiations over the past two years, we have faced scrutiny and skepticism about conservation concessions, from governments and conservationists alike. But the bold actions that some governments, together with significant financial supporters, have taken to adopt this approach indicate that it is viable both as an economic alternative and as a conservation tool.

And the idea is catching on. Last year we received a phone call from a man in Ecuador who had traveled six hours to the nearest international phone line so he could ask about establishing a conservation concession in his coastal forest community. Halfway around the world we struck up a partnership with a small non-governmental organization in Indonesia that is keen to experiment with this concept as a way to protect that nation's fragile marine ecosystems.

Now, along with other colleagues, we are looking at the feasibility of conservation concessions across Africa, Asia and Latin America, and we predict that this approach will transfer readily to many areas. If we are right, conservation concessions may indeed be able to bring to life a global market for green services.

The Authors

Jared Hardner and Richard Rice have collaborated on economic studies of biodiversity conservation in South America, Africa and Asia for the past 10 years. Hardner earned a master's degree in natural resource economics from Yale University in 1996, and four years later he co-founded Hardner & Gullison Associates, an environmental consulting firm based in Palo Alto, Calif. Rice received both a master's degree in economics and a doctorate in natural resources from the University of Michigan in 1983. In 1992 he joined Conservation International [CI], and in 1999 he accepted his current position as chief economist of the organization's Center for Applied Biodiversity Science in Washington, D.C., where Hardner also serves as a research fellow. The authors would like to express their thanks to collaborators Anita Akella, Gregory Dicum, Philip Fearnside, Sharon Flynn, Ted Gullison, Chris LaFranchi, Michelle Manion, Shelley Ratay, the staff of CI's offices in Guyana and Peru, and the staff of ProPetén in Guatemala.

Fossil fuel usage is so entrenched in the economies and infrastructures of industrialized countries that it is hard to imagine what life would be like without it. The United States alone uses 7 billion barrels of oil each year. While scientists are working on technologies to better harness energy from wind, fuel cells, the sun, and other renewable sources, movement seems to be going backward instead of forward on the government level. Officials with ties to the oil *industry, for example, wish to pursue oil drilling in the state of Alaska, which contains some of America's greatest open wilderness areas, such as the Arctic National Wildlife Refuge.*

Aside from pollution problems, fossil fuels waste a lot of money because cars, turbines, and other machines that burn them can utilize only a fraction of the energy contained in these fuels. In the following article, author Amory B. Lovins writes that coal-powered electricity works with only 3 percent efficiency when it is used to light an incandescent bulb in a home.

Lovins presents a lot of attractive possibilities and solutions to the problem. Perhaps the author's strongest evidence comes from his own home in Snowmass, Colorado, which, as its name suggests, experiences chilly winters. By installing insulation, double-paned glass, and other inexpensive indoor climate control features, he was able to eliminate the need for a conventional heating system altogether. In the future, others may follow his example, putting some of his additional suggestions to the test as well. —JV

"More Profit with Less Carbon"
by Amory B. Lovins
Scientific American, September 2005

A basic misunderstanding skews the entire climate debate. Experts on both sides claim that protecting

Earth's climate will force a trade-off between the
environment and the economy. According to these
experts, burning less fossil fuel to slow or prevent
global warming will increase the cost of meeting
society's needs for energy services, which include
everything from speedy transportation to hot showers.
Environmentalists say the cost would be modestly
higher but worth it; skeptics, including top U.S. government officials, warn that the extra expense would be
prohibitive. Yet both sides are wrong. If properly done,
climate protection would actually *reduce costs*, not
raise them. Using energy more efficiently offers an
economic bonanza—not because of the benefits of
stopping global warming but because saving fossil fuel
is a lot cheaper than buying it.

The world abounds with proven ways to use
energy more productively, and smart businesses are
leaping to exploit them. Over the past decade, chemical
manufacturer DuPont has boosted production nearly
30 percent but cut energy use 7 percent and greenhouse
gas emissions 72 percent (measured in terms of their
carbon dioxide equivalent), saving more than $2 billion
so far. Five other major firms—IBM, British Telecom,
Alcan, NorskeCanada and Bayer—have collectively
saved at least another $2 billion since the early 1990s by
reducing their carbon emissions more than 60 percent.
In 2001 oil giant BP met its 2010 goal of reducing carbon
dioxide emissions 10 percent below the company's
1990 level, thereby cutting its energy bills $650 million
over 10 years. And just this past May, General Electric

vowed to raise its energy efficiency 30 percent by 2012 to enhance the company's shareholder value. These sharp-penciled firms, and dozens like them, know that energy efficiency improves the bottom line and yields even more valuable side benefits: higher quality and reliability in energy-efficient factories, 6 to 16 percent higher labor productivity in efficient offices, and 40 percent higher sales in stores skillfully designed to be illuminated primarily by daylight.

The U.S. now uses 47 percent less energy per dollar of economic output than it did 30 years ago, lowering costs by $1 billion a day. These savings act like a huge universal tax cut that also reduces the federal deficit. Far from dampening global development, lower energy bills accelerate it. And there is plenty more value to capture at every stage of energy production, distribution and consumption. Converting coal at the power plant into incandescent light in your house is only 3 percent efficient. Most of the waste heat discarded at U.S. power stations—which amounts to 20 percent more energy than Japan uses for everything—could be lucratively recycled. About 5 percent of household electricity in the U.S. is lost to energizing computers, televisions and other appliances that are turned off. (The electricity wasted by poorly designed standby circuitry is equivalent to the output of more than a dozen 1,000-megawatt power stations running full-tilt.) In all, preventable energy waste costs Americans hundreds of billions of dollars and the global economy more than $1 trillion a year, destabilizing the climate while producing no value.

Crossroads for Energy

The Problem

- The energy sector of the global economy is woefully inefficient. Power plants and buildings waste huge amounts of heat, cars and trucks dissipate most of their fuel energy, and consumer appliances waste much of their power (and often siphon electricity even when they are turned off).
- If nothing is done, the use of oil and coal will continue to climb, draining hundreds of billions of dollars a year from the economy as well as worsening the climate, pollution and oil-security problems.

The Plan

- Improving end-use efficiency is the fastest and most lucrative way to save energy. Many energy-efficient products cost no more than inefficient ones. Homes and factories that use less power can be cheaper to build than conventional structures. Reducing the weight of vehicles can double their fuel economy without compromising safety or raising sticker prices.
- With the help of efficiency improvements and competitive renewable energy sources, the U.S. can phase out oil use by 2050. Profit-seeking businesses can lead the way.

If energy efficiency has so much potential, why isn't everyone pursuing it? One obstacle is that many people have confused efficiency (doing more with less) with curtailment, discomfort or privation (doing less, worse or without). Another obstacle is that energy users do not recognize how much they can benefit from improving efficiency, because saved energy comes in millions of invisibly small pieces, not in obvious big chunks. Most people lack the time and attention to learn about modern efficiency techniques, which evolve so quickly that even experts cannot keep up. Moreover, taxpayer-funded subsidies have made energy seem cheap. Although the U.S. government has declared that bolstering efficiency is a priority, this commitment is mostly rhetorical. And scores of ingrained rules and habits block efficiency efforts or actually reward waste. Yet relatively simple changes can turn all these obstacles into business opportunities.

Enhancing efficiency is the most vital step toward creating a climate-safe energy system, but switching to fuels that emit less carbon will also play an important role. The world economy is already decarbonizing: over the past two centuries, carbon-rich fuels such as coal have given way to fuels with less carbon (oil and natural gas) or with none (renewable sources such as solar and wind power). Today less than one third of the fossil-fuel atoms burned are carbon; the rest are climate safe hydrogen. This decarbonization trend is reinforced by greater efficiencies in converting, distributing and using energy; for example, combining the production of heat and electricity can extract twice as much useful work from each ton of carbon emitted into the atmosphere. Together these advances could dramatically reduce total carbon emissions by 2050 even as the global economy expands. This article focuses on the biggest prize: wringing more work from each unit of energy delivered to businesses and consumers. Increasing end-use efficiency can yield huge savings in fuel, pollution and capital costs because large amounts of energy are lost at every stage of the journey from production sites to delivered services [*see box on page 234*]. So even small reductions in the power used at the downstream end of the chain can enormously lower the required input at the upstream end.

The Efficiency Revolution

Many energy-efficient products, once costly and exotic, are now inexpensive and commonplace. Electronic speed controls, for example, are mass-produced so cheaply that some suppliers give them away as a free bonus with each motor. Compact fluorescent lamps cost more than $20 two decades ago but only $2 to $5 today; they use 75 to 80 percent less electricity than incandescent bulbs and last 10 to 13 times longer. Window coatings that transmit light but reflect heat cost one fourth of what they did five years ago. Indeed, for many kinds of equipment in competitive markets— motors, industrial pumps, televisions, refrigerators— some highly energy-efficient models cost no more than inefficient ones. Yet far more important than all these

Compounding Losses

From the power plant to an industrial pipe, inefficiencies along the way whittle the energy input of the fuel—set at 100 arbitrary units in this example—by more than 90 percent, leaving only 9.5 units of energy delivered as fluid flow through the pipe. But small increases in end-use efficiency can reverse these compounding losses. For instance, saving one unit of output energy by reducing friction inside the pipe will cut the needed fuel input by 10 units, slashing cost and pollution at the power plant while allowing the use of smaller, cheaper pumps and motors.

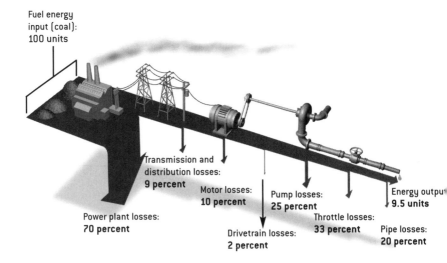

Fuel energy
input (coal):
100 units

Transmission and
distribution losses:
9 percent

Motor losses:
10 percent

Pump losses:
25 percent

Energy output
9.5 units

Power plant losses:
70 percent

Drivetrain losses:
2 percent

Throttle losses:
33 percent

Pipe losses:
20 percent

better and cheaper technologies is a hidden revolution in the design that combines and applies them.

For instance, how much thermal insulation is appropriate for a house in a cold climate? Most engineers would stop adding insulation when the expense of putting in more material rises above the savings over time from lower heating bills. But this comparison omits the capital cost of the heating system—the furnace, pipes, pumps, fans and so on—which may not be necessary at all if the insulation is good enough. Consider my own house, built in 1984 in Snowmass, Colo., where winter temperatures can dip to –44 degrees Celsius and frost can occur any day of the year. The house has no conventional heating system; instead its roof is insulated with 20 to 30 centimeters of poly- urethane foam, and its 40-centimeter-thick masonry walls sandwich another 10 centimeters of the material. The double-pane windows combine two or three trans- parent heat reflecting films with insulating krypton gas, so that they block heat as well as eight to 14 panes of glass. These features, along with heat recovery from the ventilated air, cut the house's heat losses to only about 1 percent more than the heat gained from sunlight, appliances and people inside the structure. I can offset this tiny loss by playing with my dog (who generates about 50 watts of heat, adjustable to 100 watts if you throw a ball to her) or by burning obsolete energy studies in a small woodstove on the coldest nights.

Eliminating the need for a heating system reduced construction costs by $1,100 (in 1983 dollars). I then reinvested this money, plus another $4,800, into equipment that saved half the water, 99 percent of the water-heating energy and 90 percent of the household electricity. The 4,000-square-foot structure—which also houses the original headquarters of Rocky Mountain Institute (RMI), the nonprofit group I co-founded in 1982—consumes barely more electricity than a single 100-watt lightbulb. (This amount excludes the power used by the institute's office equipment.) Solar cells generate five to six times that much electricity, which I sell back to the utility. Together all the efficiency investments repaid their cost in 10 months with 1983 technologies; today's are better and cheaper.

In the 1990s Pacific Gas & Electric undertook an experiment called ACT^2 that applied smart design in seven new and old buildings to demonstrate that large efficiency improvements can be cheaper than small ones. For example, the company built a new suburban tract house in Davis, Calif., that could stay cool in the summer without air-conditioning. PG&E estimated that such a design, if widely adopted, would cost about $1,800 less to build and $1,600 less to maintain over its lifetime than a conventional home of the same size. Similarly, in 1996 Thai architect Soontorn Boonyatikarn built a house near steamy Bangkok that required only one-seventh the air-conditioning capacity usually installed in a structure of that size; the savings in equipment costs paid for the insulating roof, walls and windows that keep the house cool [*see box on page 238*]. In all these cases, the design approach was the same:

optimize the whole building for multiple benefits rather than use isolated components for single benefits.

Such whole-system engineering can also be applied to office buildings and factories. The designers of a carpet factory built in Shanghai in 1997 cut the pumping power required for a heat-circulating loop by 92 percent through two simple changes. The first change was to install fat pipes rather than thin ones, which greatly reduced friction and hence allowed the system to use smaller pumps and motors. The second innovation was to lay out the pipes before positioning the equipment they connect. As a result, the fluid moved through short, straight pipes instead of tracing circuitous paths, further reducing friction and capital costs.

This isn't rocket science; it's just good Victorian engineering rediscovered. And it is widely applicable. A practice team at RMI has recently developed new-construction designs offering energy savings of 89 percent for a data center, about 75 percent for a chemical plant, 70 to 90 percent for a supermarket and about 50 percent for a luxury yacht, all with capital costs lower than those of conventional designs. The team has also proposed retrofits for existing oil refineries, mines and microchip factories that would reduce energy use by 40 to 60 percent, repaying their cost in just a few years.

Vehicles of Opportunity

Transportation consumes 70 percent of U.S. oil and generates a third of the nation's carbon emissions. It is

Saving Energy by Design

How can you keep cool in tropical Thailand while mini-mizing power usage? Architect Soontorn Boonyatikarn of Chulalongkorn University used overhangs and balconies to shade his 350-square-meter home in Pathumthani, near Bangkok. Insulation, an airtight shell and infrared-reflecting windows keep heat out of the house while letting in plenty of daylight. An open floor plan and central stairwell promote ventilation, and indoor air is cooled as it flows through an underground tube. As a result, the house needs just one seventh of the typical air-conditioning capacity for a structure of its size. To further reduce energy bills, the air-conditioning system's condensers heat the house's water.

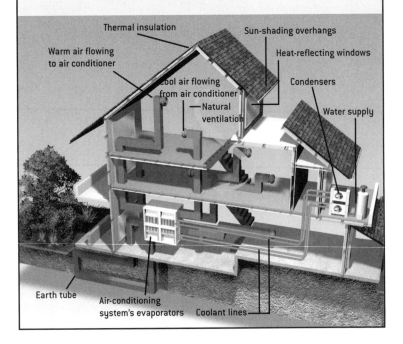

Thermal insulation

Sun-shading overhangs

Warm air flowing
to air conditioner

Heat-reflecting windows

Cool air flowing
from air conditioner

Condensers

Natural
ventilation

Water supply

Earth tube

Air-conditioning
system's evaporators

Coolant lines

widely considered the most intractable part of the climate problem, especially as hundreds of millions of people in China and India buy automobiles. Yet transportation offers enormous efficiency opportunities. *Winning the Oil Endgame*, a 2004 analysis written by my team at RMI and co-sponsored by the Pentagon, found that artfully combining lightweight materials with innovations in propulsion and aerodynamics could cut oil use by cars, trucks and planes by two thirds without compromising comfort, safety, performance or affordability.

Despite 119 years of refinement, the modern car remains astonishingly inefficient. Only 13 percent of its fuel energy even reaches the wheels—the other 87 percent is either dissipated as heat and noise in the engine and drivetrain or lost to idling and accessories such as air conditioners. Of the energy delivered to the wheels, more than half heats the tires, road and air. Just 6 percent of the fuel energy actually accelerates the car (and all this energy converts to brake heating when you stop). And, because 95 percent of the accelerated mass is the car itself, less than 1 percent of the fuel ends up moving the driver.

Yet the solution is obvious from the physics: greatly reduce the car's weight, which causes three fourths of the energy losses at the wheels. And every unit of energy saved at the wheels by lowering weight (or cutting drag) will save an additional seven units of energy now lost en route to the wheels. Concerns about cost and safety have long discouraged attempts to make lighter cars, but modern light-but-strong materials—new metal alloys and advanced polymer composites—can slash a car's mass without sacrificing crashworthiness. For example, carbon-fiber composites can absorb six to 12 times as much crash energy per kilogram as steel does, more than offsetting the composite car's weight disadvantage if it hits a steel vehicle that is twice as heavy. With such novel materials, cars can be big, comfortable and protective without being heavy, inefficient and hostile, saving both oil *and* lives. As Henry Ford said, you don't need weight for strength; if you did, your bicycle helmet would be made of steel, not carbon fiber.

Advanced manufacturing techniques developed in the past two years could make carbon-composite car bodies competitive with steel ones. A lighter body would allow automakers to use smaller (and less expensive) engines. And because the assembly of carbon-composite cars does not require body or paint shops, the factories would be smaller and cost 40 percent less to build than conventional auto plants. These savings would offset the higher cost of the carbon-composite materials. In all, the introduction of ultralight bodies could nearly double the fuel efficiency of today's hybrid-electric vehicles—which are already twice as efficient as conventional cars—without raising their sticker prices. If composites prove unready, new ultralight steels offer a reliable backstop. The competitive marketplace will sort out the winning materials, but, either way, super efficient ultralight vehicles will start pulling away from the automotive pack within the next decade.

What is more, ultralight cars could greatly accelerate the transition to hydrogen fuel-cell cars that use no oil at all. A midsize SUV whose halved weight and drag cut its needed power to the wheels by two thirds would have a fuel economy equivalent to 114 miles per gallon and thus require only a 35-kilowatt fuel cell— one third the usual size and hence much easier to manufacture affordably [*see box on page 244*]. And because the vehicle would need to carry only one third as much hydrogen, it would not require any new storage technologies; compact, safe, off-the-shelf carbon-fiber tanks could hold enough hydrogen to propel the SUV for 530 kilometers. Thus, the first automaker to go ultralight will win the race to fuel cells, giving the whole industry a strong incentive to become as boldly innovative in materials and manufacturing as a few companies now are in propulsion.

RMI's analysis shows that full adoption of efficient vehicles, buildings and industries could shrink projected U.S. oil use in 2025—28 million barrels a day—by more than half, lowering consumption to pre-1970 levels. In a realistic scenario, only about half of these savings could actually be captured by 2025 because many older, less efficient cars and trucks would remain on the road (vehicle stocks turn over slowly). Before 2050, though, U.S. oil consumption could be phased out altogether by doubling the efficiency of oil use and substituting alternative fuel supplies. Businesses can profit greatly by making the transition, because saving each barrel of oil through efficiency improvements costs only \$12, less than one fifth of what petroleum sells for today. And two kinds of alternative fuel supplies could compete robustly with oil even if it sold for less than half the current price. The first is ethanol made from woody, weedy plants such as switchgrass and poplar. Corn is currently the main U.S. source of ethanol, which is blended with gasoline, but the woody plants yield twice as much ethanol per ton as corn does and with lower capital investment and far less energy input.

The second alternative is replacing oil with lower-carbon natural gas, which would become cheaper and more abundant as efficiency gains reduce the demand for electricity at peak periods. At those times, gas-fired turbines generate power so wastefully that saving 1 percent of electricity would cut U.S. natural gas consumption by 2 percent and its price by 3 or 4 percent. Gas saved in this way and in other uses could then replace oil either directly or, even more profitably and efficiently, by converting it to hydrogen.

The benefits of phasing out oil would go far beyond the estimated \$70 billion saved every year. The transition would lower U.S. carbon emissions by 26 percent and eliminate all the social and political costs of getting and burning petroleum—military conflict, price volatility, fiscal and diplomatic distortions, pollution and so on. If the country becomes oil-free, then petroleum will no longer be worth fighting over. The Pentagon would also reap immediate rewards from raising energy efficiency because it badly needs to reduce the costs and risks of supplying fuel to its troops. Just as the U.S. Department of Defense's research efforts transformed civilian industry by creating the Internet and the Global Positioning System, it should now spearhead the development of advanced ultralight materials.

The switch to an oil-free economy would happen even faster than RMI projected if policymakers stopped encouraging the perverse development patterns that make people drive so much. If federal, state and local governments did not mandate and subsidize sub-urban sprawl, more of us could live in neighborhoods where almost everything we want is within a five-minute walk. Besides saving fuel, this New Urbanist design builds stronger communities, earns more money for developers and is much less disruptive than other methods of limiting vehicle traffic (such as the draconian fuel and car taxes that Singapore uses to avoid Bangkok-like traffic jams).

Renewable Energy

Efficiency improvements that can save most of our electricity also cost less than what the utilities now pay for coal, which generates half of U.S. power and 38 percent of its fossil-fuel carbon emissions. Furthermore, in recent years alternatives to coal-fired power plants—including renewable sources such as wind and solar power, as well as decentralized cogeneration plants that produce electricity and heat together in buildings and factories—have begun to hit their stride.

A Lean, Mean Driving Machine

Ultralight cars can be fast, roomy, safe and efficient. A concept five-seat midsize SUV called the Revolution, designed in 2000, weighs only 857 kilograms—less than half the weight of a comparable conventional car—yet its carbon-fiber safety cell would protect passengers from high-speed collisions with much heavier vehicles. A 35-kilowatt fuel cell could propel the car for 530 kilometers on 3.4 kilograms of hydrogen stored in its tanks. And the Revolution could accelerate to 100 kilometers per hour in 8.3 seconds.

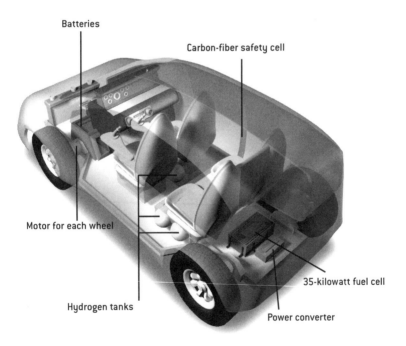

Batteries

Carbon-fiber safety cell

Motor for each wheel

35-kilowatt fuel cell

Hydrogen tanks

Power converter

Worldwide the collective generating capacity of these sources is already greater than that of nuclear power and growing six times as fast. This trend is all the more impressive because decentralized generators face many obstacles to fair competition and usually get much lower subsidies than centralized coal-fired or nuclear plants.

Wind power is perhaps the greatest success story. Mass production and improved engineering have made modern wind turbines big (generating two to five megawatts each), extremely reliable and environmentally quite benign. Denmark already gets a fifth of its electricity from wind, Germany a tenth. Germany and Spain are each adding more than 2,000 megawatts of wind power each year, and Europe aims to get 22 percent of its electricity and 12 percent of its total energy from renewables by 2010. In contrast, global nuclear generating capacity is expected to remain flat, then decline.

The most common criticism of wind power—that it produces electricity too intermittently—has not turned out to be a serious drawback. In parts of Europe that get all their power from wind on some days, utilities have overcome the problem by diversifying the locations of their wind turbines, incorporating wind forecasts into their generating plans and integrating wind power with hydroelectricity and other energy sources. Wind and solar power work particularly well together, partly because the conditions that are bad for wind (calm, sunny weather) are good for solar, and vice versa. In fact, when properly combined, wind and solar facilities are more reliable than conventional power stations—they come in smaller modules (wind turbines, solar cells) that are less likely to fail all at once, their costs do not swing wildly with the prices of fossil fuels, and terrorists are much more likely to attack a nuclear reactor or an oil terminal than a wind farm or a solar array.

Most important, renewable power now has advantageous economics. In 2003 U.S. wind energy sold for as little as 2.9 cents a kilowatt-hour. The federal government subsidizes wind power with a production tax credit, but even without that subsidy, the price—about 4.6 cents per kilowatt-hour—is still cheaper than subsidized power from new coal or nuclear plants. (Wind power's subsidy is a temporary one that Congress has repeatedly allowed to expire; in contrast, the subsidies for the fossil-fuel and nuclear industries are larger and permanent.) Wind power is also abundant: wind farms occupying just a few percent of the available land in the Dakotas could cost-effectively meet all of America's electricity needs. Although solar cells currently cost more per kilowatt-hour than wind turbines do, they can still be profitable if integrated into buildings, saving the cost of roofing materials. Atop big, flat-roofed commercial buildings, solar cells can compete without subsidies if combined with efficient use that allows the building's owner to resell the surplus power when it is most plentiful and valuable—on sunny afternoons. Solar is also usually the cheapest way to get electricity to the two billion people, mostly in the developing world, who have no access to power lines. But even in rich countries, a house as efficient as mine can get all its electricity from just a few square meters of solar cells, and installing the array costs less than connecting to nearby utility lines.

Cheaper to Fix

Inexpensive efficiency improvements and competitive renewable sources can reverse the terrible arithmetic of climate change, which accelerates exponentially as we burn fossil fuels ever faster. Efficiency can outpace economic growth if we pay attention: between 1977 and 1985, for example, U.S. gross domestic product (GDP) grew 27 percent, whereas oil use fell 17 percent. (Over the same period, oil imports dropped 50 percent, and Persian Gulf imports plummeted 87 percent.) The growth of renewables has routinely outpaced GDP; worldwide, solar and wind power are doubling every two and three years, respectively. If both efficiency and renewables grow faster than the economy, then carbon emissions will fall and global warming will slow— buying more time to develop even better technologies for displacing the remaining fossil-fuel use, or to master and deploy ways to capture combustion carbon before it enters the air.

In contrast, nuclear power is a slower and much more expensive solution. Delivering a kilowatt-hour from a new nuclear plant costs at least three times as much as saving one through efficiency measures. Thus, every dollar spent on efficiency would displace at least three times as much coal as spending on nuclear power, and the efficiency improvements could go into effect much more quickly because it takes so long to build reactors. Diverting public and private investment from market winners to losers does not just distort markets and misallocate financial capital—it worsens the climate problem by buying a less effective solution.

The good news about global warming is that it is cheaper to fix than to ignore. Because saving energy is profitable, efficient use is gaining traction in the marketplace. U.S. Environmental Protection Agency economist Skip Laitner calculates that from 1996 to mid-2005 prudent choices by businesses and consumers, combined with the shift to a more information and service-based economy, cut average U.S. energy use per dollar of GDP by 2.1 percent a year—nearly three times as fast as the rate for the preceding 10 years. This change met 78 percent of the rise in demand for energy services over the past decade (the remainder was met by increasing energy supply), and the U.S. achieved this progress without the help of any techno-logical breakthroughs or new national policies. The climate problem was created by millions of bad decisions over decades, but climate stability can be restored by millions of sensible choices—buying a more efficient lamp or car, adding insulation or caulk to your home, repealing subsidies for waste and rewarding desired outcomes (for example, by paying architects and engineers for savings, not expenditures).

The proper role of government is to steer, not row, but for years officials have been steering our energy ship in the wrong direction. The current U.S. energy policy harms the economy and the climate by rejecting free-market principles and playing favorites with technologies. The best course is to allow every method of producing or saving energy to compete fairly, at honest prices, regardless of which kind of investment it is, what technology it uses, how big it is or who owns it. For example, few jurisdictions currently let decentralized power sources such as rooftop solar arrays "plug and play" on the electric grid, as modern technical standards safely permit. Although 31 U.S. states allow net metering—the utility buys your power at the same price it charges you—most artificially restrict or distort this competition. But the biggest single obstacle to electric and gas efficiency is that most countries, and all U.S. states except California and Oregon, reward distribution utilities for selling more energy and penalize them for cutting their customers' bills. Luckily, this problem is easy to fix: state regulators should align incentives by decoupling profits from energy sales, then letting utilities keep some of the savings from trimming energy bills.

Superefficient vehicles have been slow to emerge from Detroit, where neither balance sheets nor leadership has supported visionary innovation. Also, the U.S. lightly taxes gasoline but heavily subsidizes its production, making it cheaper than bottled water. Increasing fuel taxes may not be the best solution, though; in Europe, stiff taxes—which raise many countries' gasoline prices to $4 or $5 a gallon—cut driving more than they make new cars efficient, because fuel costs are diluted by car owners' other expenses and are then steeply discounted (most car buyers count only the first few years' worth of fuel savings). Federal standards adopted in the 1970s helped to lift the fuel economy of new cars and light trucks from 16 miles per gallon in 1978 to 22 miles per gallon in 1987, but the average has slipped to 21 mpg since then. The government projects that the auto industry will spend the next 20 years getting its vehicles to be just 0.5 mile per gallon more efficient than they were in 1987. Furthermore, automakers loathe the standards as restrictions on choice and have become adept at gaming the system by selling more vehicles classified as light trucks, which are allowed to have lower fuel economy than cars. (The least efficient light trucks even get special subsidies.)

The most powerful policy response is "feebates"—charging fees on inefficient new cars and returning that revenue as rebates to buyers of efficient models. If done separately for each size class of vehicle, so there is no bias against bigger models, feebates would expand customer choice instead of restricting it. Feebates would also encourage innovation, save customers money and boost automakers' profits. Such policies, which can be implemented at the state level, could speed the adoption of advanced-technology cars, trucks and planes without mandates, taxes, subsidies or new national laws.

In Europe and Japan, the main obstacle to saving energy is the mistaken belief that their economies are already as efficient as they can get. These countries are up to twice as efficient as the U.S., but they still have a long way to go. The greatest opportunities, though, are in developing countries, which are on average three times less efficient than the U.S. Dreadfully wasteful motors, lighting ballasts and other devices are freely traded and widely bought in these nations. Their power sector currently devours one quarter of their development funds, diverting money from other vital projects. Industrial countries are partly responsible for this situation because many have exported inefficient vehicles and equipment to the developing world. Exporting inefficiency is both immoral and uneconomic; instead the richer nations should help developing countries build an energy-efficient infrastructure that would free up capital to address their other pressing needs. For example, manufacturing efficient lamps and windows takes 1,000 times less capital than building power plants and grids to do the same tasks, and the investment is recovered 10 times faster.

China and India have already discovered that their burgeoning economies cannot long compete if energy waste continues to squander their money, talent and public health. China is setting ambitious but achievable goals for shifting from coal-fired power to decentralized renewable energy and natural gas. (The Chinese have large supplies of gas and are expected to tap vast reserves in eastern Siberia.) Moreover, in 2004 China announced an energy strategy built around "leapfrog technologies" and rapid improvements in the efficiency of new buildings, factories and consumer products. China is also taking steps to control the explosive growth of its oil use; by 2008 it will be illegal to sell many inefficient U.S. cars there. If American automakers do not innovate quickly enough, in another decade you may well be driving a superefficient Chinese-made car. A million U.S. jobs hang in the balance.

Today's increasingly competitive global economy is stimulating an exciting new pattern of energy investment. If governments can remove institutional barriers and harness the dynamism of free enterprise, the markets will naturally favor choices that generate wealth, protect the climate and build real security by replacing fossil fuels with cheaper alternatives. This technology-driven convergence of business, environmental and security interests—creating abundance by design—holds out the promise of a fairer, richer and safer world.

The Author

Amory B. Lovins is co-founder and chief executive of Rocky Mountain Institute, an entrepreneurial nonprofit organization based in Snowmass, Colo., and chairman of Fiberforge, an engineering firm in Glenwood Springs, Colo. A physicist, Lovins has consulted for industry and governments worldwide for more than 30 years, chiefly on energy and its links with the environment, development and security. He has published 29 books and hundreds of papers on these subjects and has received a MacArthur Fellowship and many other awards for his work.

Curitiba is a large and not particularly wealthy city in Brazil. One would expect it to have all of the typical problems of modern urban life, such as traffic, pollution, and high crime. Instead, Curitiba has managed to escape these problems with the help of visionary leadership and careful planning.

One of the biggest improvements Brazilian leaders made was to design the city so that traffic can flow through it via multiple roads instead of collecting in a handful of congested freeways. Since public transportation fully services these roads and is well maintained, most people do not commute in individual cars. Leaders also created extensive recycling programs with incentives for the public, especially people in poor neighborhoods, to eliminate garbage and to recycle whenever possible.

The authors of the following article believe that Curitiba stands as a model city that should inspire better urban planning in many other countries. People there realized that problems are not "specific and isolated but

*rather interconnected." That logic could apply to
all of the subjects addressed in this anthology,
from global warming to animal extinctions.
Problems related to these issues involve and
affect many different players, including us. It is
in our best interest to try to resolve these issues
now, as Curitiba's leaders did. —JV*

"Urban Planning in Curitiba"
by Jonas Rabinovitch and Josef Leitman
Scientific American, March 1996

As late as the end of the 19th century, even a visionary
like Jules Verne could not imagine a city with more
than a million inhabitants. Yet by the year 2010 over
500 such concentrations will dot the globe, 26 of them
with more than 10 million people. Indeed, for the first
time in history more people now live in cities than in
rural areas.

Most modern cities have developed to meet the
demands of the automobile. Private transport has
affected the physical layout of cities, the location of
housing, commerce and industries, and the patterns
of human interaction. Urban planners design around
highways, parking structures and rush-hour traffic
patterns. And urban engineers attempt to control
nature within the confines of the city limits, often at
the expense of environmental concerns. Cities traditionally deploy technological solutions to solve a
variety of challenges, such as drainage or pollution.

Curitiba, the capital of Paraná state in southeastern Brazil, has taken a different path. One of the fastest-growing cities in a nation of urban booms, its metropolitan area mushroomed from 300,000 citizens in 1950 to 2.1 million in 1990. Curitiba's economic base has changed radically during this period: once a center for processing agricultural products, it has become an industrial and commercial powerhouse. The consequences of such rapid change are familiar to students of Third World development: unemployment, squatter settlements, congestion, environmental decay. But Curitiba did not end up like many of its sister cities. Instead, although its poverty and income profile is typical of the region, it has significantly less pollution, a slightly lower crime rate and a higher educational level among its citizens.

Designing with Nature

Why did Curitiba succeed where others have faltered? Progressive city administrations turned Curitiba into a living laboratory for a style of urban development based on a preference for public transportation over the private automobile, working with the environment instead of against it, appropriate rather than high-technology solutions, and innovation with citizen participation in place of master planning. This philosophy was gradually institutionalized during the late 1960s and officially adopted in 1971 by a visionary mayor, Jaime Lerner, who was also an architect and planner. The past 25 years have shown that it was the right choice; Rafael Greca, the current mayor, has continued the policies of past administrations and built on them.

One of Curitiba's first successes was in controlling the persistent flooding that plagued the city center during the 1950s and early 1960s. Construction of houses and other structures along the banks of streams and rivers had exacerbated the problem. Civil engineers had covered many streams, converting them into underground canals that made drainage even more difficult—additional drainage canals had to be excavated at enormous cost. At the same time, developers were building new neighborhoods and industrial districts on the periphery of the city without proper attention to drainage.

Beginning in 1966 the city set aside strips of land for drainage and put certain low-lying areas off-limits for building. In 1975 stringent legislation was enacted to protect the remaining natural drainage system. To make use of these areas, Curitiba turned many river-banks into parks, building artificial lakes to contain floodwaters. The parks have been extensively planted with trees, and disused factories and other streamside buildings have been recycled into sports and leisure facilities. Buses and bicycle paths integrate the parks with the city's transportation system.

This "design with nature" strategy has solved several problems at the same time. It has made the costly flooding a thing of the past even while it allowed the city to forgo substantial new investments in flood control. Perhaps even more important, the use of otherwise treacherous floodplains for parkland has enabled Curitiba to increase the amount of green space per capita from half a square meter in 1970 to 50 today—during a period of rapid population growth.

Priority to Public Transport

Perhaps the most obvious sign that Curitiba differs from other cities is the absence of a gridlocked center fed by overcrowded highways. Most cities grow in a concentric fashion, annexing new districts around the outside while progressively increasing the density of the commercial and business districts at their core. Congestion is inevitable, especially if most commuters travel from the periphery to the center in private automobiles. During the 1970s, Curitiba authorities instead emphasized growth along prescribed structural axes, allowing the city to spread out while developing mass transit that kept shops, workplaces and homes readily accessible to one another. Curitiba's road network and public transport system are probably the most influential elements accounting for the shape of the city.

Each of the five main axes along which the city has grown consists of three parallel roadways. The central road contains two express bus lanes flanked by local roads; one block away to either side run high-capacity one-way streets heading into and out of the central city. Land-use legislation has encouraged high-density occupation, together with services and commerce, in the areas adjacent to each axis.

The city augmented these spatial changes with a bus-based public transportation system designed for convenience and speed. Interdistrict and feeder bus routes complement the express bus lanes along the structural axes. Large bus terminals at the far ends of the five express bus lanes permit transfers from one route to another, as do medium-size terminals located approximately every two kilometers along the express routes. A single fare allows passengers to transfer from the express routes to interdistrict and local buses.

The details of the system are designed for speed and simplicity just as much as the overall architecture. Special raised-tube bus stops, where passengers pay their fares in advance (as in a subway station), speed boarding, as do the two extra-wide doors on each bus. This combination has cut total travel time by a third. Curitiba also runs double- and triple-length articulated buses that increase the capacity of the express bus lanes.

Ironically, the reasoning behind the choice of transportation technology was not only efficiency but also simple economics: to build a subway system would have cost roughly $60 million to $70 million per kilometer; the express bus highways came in at $200,000 per kilometer including the boarding tubes. Bus operation and maintenance were also familiar tasks that the private sector could carry out. Private companies, following guidance and parameters established by the city administration, are responsible for all mass transit in Curitiba. Bus companies are paid by the number of kilometers that they operate rather than by the number of passengers they transport, allowing a balanced distribution of bus routes and eliminating destructive competition.

As a result of this system, average low-income residents of Curitiba spend only about 10 percent of their income on transport, which is relatively low for Brazil. Although the city has more than 500,000 private cars (more cars per capita than any Brazilian city except the capital, Brasília), three quarters of all commuters—more than 1.3 million passengers a day—take the bus. Per capita fuel consumption is 25 percent lower than in comparable Brazilian cities, and Curitiba has one of the lowest rates of ambient air pollution in the country. Although the buses run on diesel fuel, the number of car trips they eliminate more than makes up for their emissions.

In addition to these benefits, the city has a self-financing public transportation system, instead of being saddled by debt to pay for the construction and operating subsidies that a subway system entails. The savings have been invested in other areas. (Even old buses do not go to waste: they provide transportation to parks or serve as mobile schools.)

The implementation of the public transport system also allowed the development of a low-income housing program that provided some 40,000 new dwellings. Before implementing the public transport system, the city purchased and set aside land for low-income housing near the Curitiba Industrial City, a manufacturing

district founded in 1972, located about eight kilometers
west of the city center. Because the value of land is
largely determined by its proximity to transportation
and other facilities, these "land stocks" made it possible
for the poor to have homes with ready access to jobs in
an area where housing prices would otherwise have
been unaffordable. The Curitiba Industrial City now
supports 415 companies that directly and indirectly
generate one fifth of all jobs in the city; polluting
industries are not allowed.

Participation Through Incentives

The city managers of Curitiba have learned that good
systems and incentives are as important as good plans.
The city's master plan helped to forge a vision and
strategic principles to guide future developments. The
vision was transformed into reality, however, by
reliance on the right systems and incentives, not on
slavish implementation of a static document.

One such innovative system is the provision of
public information about land. City Hall can immediately deliver information to any citizen about the
building potential of any plot in the city. Anyone
wishing to obtain or renew a business permit must
provide information to project impacts on traffic, infrastructure needs, parking requirements and municipal
concerns. Ready access to this information helps to
avoid land speculation; it has also been essential for
budgetary purposes, because property taxes are the
city's main source of revenue.

Incentives have been important in reinforcing positive behavior. Owners of land in the city's historic district can transfer the building potential of their plots to another area of the city—a rule that works to preserve historic buildings while fairly compensating their owners. In addition, businesses in specified areas throughout the city can "buy" permission to build up to two extra floors beyond the legal limit. Payment can be made in the form of cash or land that the city then uses to fund low-income housing.

Incentives and systems for encouraging beneficial behavior also work at the individual level. Curitiba's Free University for the Environment offers practical short courses at no cost for homemakers, building superintendents, shopkeepers and others to teach the environmental implications of the daily routines of even the most commonplace jobs. The courses, taught by people who have completed an appropriate training program, are a prerequisite for licenses to work at some jobs, such as taxi driving, but many other people take them voluntarily.

The city also funds a number of important programs for children, putting money behind the often empty pronouncements municipalities make about the importance of the next generation. The Paperboy/Papergirl Program gives part-time jobs to schoolchildren from low-income families; municipal day care centers serve four meals a day for some 12,000 children; and SOS Children provides a special telephone number for urgent communications about children under any kind of threat.

Integrated Design Makes Busways Work

Curitiba's express bus system is designed as a single entity, rather than as disparate components of buses, stops and roads. As a result, the busways borrow many features from the subway system that the city might otherwise have built, had it a few billion dollars to spare. Most urban bus systems require passengers to pay as they board, slowing loading. Curitiba's raised-tube bus stops eliminate this step: passengers pay as they enter the tube, and so the bus spends more of its time actually moving people from place to place.

Similarly, the city installed wheelchair lifts at bus stops rather than onboard buses, easing weight restrictions and simplifying maintenance—buses with built-in wheelchair lifts are notoriously trouble-prone, as are those that "kneel" to put their boarding steps within reach of the elderly. The tube-stop lifts also speed boarding by bringing disabled passengers to the proper height before the bus arrives.

Like subways, the buses have a track dedicated entirely to their use. This right-of-way significantly reduces travel time compared with buses that must fight automotive traffic to reach their destinations. By putting concrete and asphalt above the ground instead of excavating to place steel rails underneath it, however, the city managed to achieve most of the goals that subways strive for at less than 5 percent of the initial cost.

Some of the savings have enabled Curitiba to keep its fleet of 2,000 buses—owned by 10 private companies under contract to the city—among the newest in the world. The average bus is only three years old. The city pays bus owners 1 percent of the value of a bus each month; after 10 years it takes possession of retired vehicles and refurbishes them as free park buses or mobile schools.

Companies are paid according to the length of the routes they serve rather than the number of passengers they carry, giving the city a strong incentive to provide service that increases ridership. Indeed, more than a quarter of Curitiba's automobile owners take the bus to work. In response to increased demand, the city has augmented the capacity of its busways by using extra-long buses—the equivalent of multicar subway trains. The biarticulated bus, in service since 1992, has three sections connected by hinges that allow it to turn corners. At full capacity, these vehicles can carry 270 passengers, more than three times as many as an ordinary bus. —*J. R.*

Curitiba has repeatedly rejected conventional wisdom that emphasizes technologically sophisticated solutions to urban woes. Many planners have contended, for example, that cities with over a million people must have a subway system to avoid traffic congestion. Prevailing dogma also claims that cities that generate more than 1,000 tons of solid waste a day need expensive mechanical garbage-separation plants. Yet Curitiba has neither.

The city has attacked the solid-waste issue from both the generation and collection sides. Citizens recycle paper equivalent to nearly 1,200 trees each day. The Garbage That Is Not Garbage initiative has drawn more than 70 percent of households to sort recyclable materials for collection. The Garbage Purchase program, designed specifically for low-income areas, helps to clean up sites that are difficult for the conventional waste-management system to serve. Poor families can exchange filled garbage bags for bus tokens, parcels of surplus food and children's school notebooks. More than 34,000 families in 62 poor neighborhoods have exchanged over 11,000 tons of garbage for nearly a million bus tokens and 1,200 tons of surplus food. During the past three years, students in more than 100 schools have traded nearly 200 tons of garbage for close to 1.9 million notebooks. Another initiative, All Clean, temporarily hires retired and unemployed people to clean up specific areas of the city where litter has accumulated.

These innovations, which rely on public participation and labor-intensive approaches rather than on mechanization and massive capital investment, have reduced the cost and increased the effectiveness of the city's solid-waste management system. They have also conserved resources, beautified the city and provided employment.

Lessons for an Urbanizing World

No other city has precisely the combination of geographic, economic and political conditions that mark Curitiba. Nevertheless, its successes can serve as lessons for urban planners in both the industrial and the developing worlds.

Perhaps the most important lesson is that top priority should be given to public transport rather than to private cars and to pedestrians rather than to motorized vehicles. Bicycle paths and pedestrian areas should be an integrated part of the road network and public transportation system. Whereas intensive road-building programs elsewhere have led paradoxically to even more congestion, Curitiba's slighting of the needs of private motorized traffic has generated less use of cars and has reduced pollution.

Curitiba's planners have also learned that solutions to urban problems are not specific and isolated but rather interconnected. Any plan should involve partnerships among private-sector entrepreneurs, nongovernmental organizations, municipal agencies, utilities, neighborhood associations, community groups and individuals. Creative and labor-intensive ideas—especially where unemployment is already a problem—can often substitute for conventional capital-intensive technologies.

We have found that cities can turn traditional sources of problems into resources. For example, public transport, urban solid waste, and unemployment are traditionally considered problems, but they have the potential to become generators of new resources, as they have in Curitiba.

Other cities are beginning to learn some of these lessons. In Brazil and elsewhere in Latin America, the pedestrian streets that Curitiba pioneered have become popular urban fixtures. Cape Town has recently developed a new vision for its metropolitan area that is explicitly based on Curitiba's system of structural axes. Officials and planners from places as diverse as New York City, Toronto, Montreal, Paris, Lyons, Moscow, Prague, Santiago, Buenos Aires and Lagos have visited the city and praised it.

As these planners carry Curitiba's examples back to their homes, they also come away with a crucial principle: there is no time like the present. Rather than trying to revitalize urban centers that have begun falling into decay, planners in already large cities and those that have just started to grow can begin solving problems without waiting for top-down master plans or near fiscal collapse.

The Authors

Jonas Rabinovitch and Josef Leitman are urban planners, Rabinovitch at the United Nations and Leitman at the World Bank. Rabinovitch earned his bachelor's degree in architecture and urban planning from the Federal University of Rio de Janeiro and received a master's degree in the economics of urban development from University College London, with a specialization in urban traffic and transport planning. Before coming to the U.N. three years ago, he was an adviser to the mayor and director of international relations for Curitiba, having joined the city's research and urban planning institute in 1981. Leitman is a senior urban planner at the World Bank. He received his doctorate in city and regional planning from the University of California, Berkeley, in 1992. He earned bachelor's and master's degrees from Harvard University. This article reflects the opinions of the authors, not necessarily those of the city of Curitiba, the United Nations Development Program or the World Bank.

Web Sites

Due to the changing nature of Internet links, the Rosen Publishing Group, Inc., has developed an online list of Web sites related to the subject of this book. This site is updated regularly. Please use this link to access the list:

http://www.rosenlinks.com/saca/plea

For Further Reading

Cohen, Joel E. *How Many People Can the Earth Support?* New York, NY: W. W. Norton, 1995.

Erickson, Jon. *Lost Creatures of the Earth: Mass Extinction in the History of Life.* New York, NY: Facts on File, 2001.

Fagan, Brian. *The Little Ice Age: How Climate Made History, 1300–1850.* New York, NY: Basic Books, 2003.

Fridell, Ron. *Global Warming*. New York, NY: Scholastic Library Publishing, 2002.

Green, Kenneth. *Global Warming: Understanding the Debate*. Berkeley Heights, NJ: Enslow, 2002.

Lynas, Mark. *High Tide: The Truth About Our Climate Crisis*. New York, NY: Picador, 2004.

Munoz, William. *Biodiversity*. New York, NY: Houghton Mifflin Company, 1996.

Quammen, David. *The Song of the Dodo: Island Biogeography in an Age of Extinctions*. New York, NY: Scribner, 1996.

Safina, Carl. *Eye of the Albatross: Visions of Hope and Survival*. New York, NY: Henry Holt, 2002.

Schneiderman, Jill S., ed. *The Earth Around Us: Maintaining a Livable Planet*. New York, NY: W. H. Freeman, 2000.

Shiva, Vandana. *Water Wars: Privatization, Pollution, and Profit*. Cambridge, MA: South End Press, 2002.

Silverstein, Alvin. *Global Warming*. Minneapolis, MN: Lerner Publishing Group, 2003.

Wilson, Edward O. *The Future of Life*. New York, NY: Alfred A. Knopf, 2002.

Zeaman, John. *Overpopulation*. New York, NY: Scholastic Library Publishing, 2002.

Bibliography

Bindschadler, Robert A., and Charles R. Bentley. "On Thin Ice?" *Scientific American*, Vol. 287, No. 6, December 2002, pp. 98–105.

Blaustein, Andrew R., and David B. Wake. "The Puzzle of Declining Amphibian Populations." *Scientific American*, Vol. 272, No. 4, April 1995, pp. 52–57.

Cohen, Joel E. "Human Population Grows Up." *Scientific American*, Vol. 293, No. 3, September 2005, pp. 48–55.

Dasgupta, Partha S. "Population, Poverty and the Local Environment." *Scientific American*, Vol. 272, No. 2, February 1995, pp. 40–45.

Frosch, Robert A. "The Industrial Ecology of the 21st Century." *Scientific American*, Vol. 273, No. 3, September 1995, pp. 178–181.

Gibbs, W. Wayt. "On the Termination of Species." *Scientific American*, Vol. 285, No. 5, November 2001, pp. 40–49.

Gleick, Peter H. "Making Every Drop Count." *Scientific American*, Vol. 284, No. 2, February 2001, pp. 41–45.

Grossman, Daniel. "Spring Forward." *Scientific American*, Vol. 290, No.1, January 2004, pp. 85–91.

Hardner, Jared, and Richard Rice. "Rethinking Green
Consumerism." *Scientific American,* Vol. 286, No. 5,
May 2002, pp. 89–95.

Homer-Dixon, Thomas F., Jeffrey H. Boutwell, and
George W. Rathjens. "Environmental Change and
Violent Conflict." *Scientific American,* Vol. 268,
No. 2, February 1993, pp. 38–45.

Lovins, Amory B. "More Profit with Less Carbon."
Scientific American, Vol. 293, No. 3, September
2005, pp. 74–83.

Rabinovitch, Jonas, and Josef Leitman. "Urban Planning
in Curitiba." *Scientific American,* Vol. 274, No. 3,
March 1996, pp. 46–53.

Safina, Carl. "The World's Imperiled Fish." *Scientific
American Presents: The Oceans,* Vol. 9, No. 3, 1998,
pp. 58–63.

Tattersall, Ian. "Madagascar's Lemurs." *Scientific
American,* Vol. 268, No. 1, January 1993,
pp. 110–117.

Index

Z

About the Editor

Jennifer Viegas is a reporter for the Australian Broadcasting Corporation and Discovery News, the news service for the Discovery Channel and Animal Planet. She is the author of several reports on climate change that were published by Physicians for Social Responsibility, a Washington D.C.–based public policy organization. Data quoted in these reports was mentioned during the debates for the 2000 presidential election, which she covered. She secured private interviews with both former vice president Al Gore and current president George W. Bush. She also has served as a news columnist for Knight Ridder newspapers and has written educational materials for the *Princeton Review*.

Illustration Credits

Cover: Dado Galdieri/AP; p. 15 Nadia Strasser; p. 22 Nadia Strasser (Source: Marcel E. Visser, Christiaan Both and Marcel M. Lambrechts); p. 52 Johnny Johnson (Source: Peter H. Gleick); p. 75 Patricia J. Wynne; pp. 86–87, 95 Laurie Grace (Source: Food and Agriculture Organization); p. 92 Laurie Grace (graph), Roberto Osti (drawings) (Source: National Marine Fisheries Service); p. 93 Laurie Grace (graph) (Source: Food and Agriculture Organization); pp. 161, 168 Lisa Burnett; p. 180 Jared Scheidman Design; pp. 183, 194 Jared Scheidman Design (Source: World Resources Institute); p. 191 Jared Scheidman Design (Source: Peter H. Gleick, Pacific Institute, Oakland, Calif.); pp. 234, 238, 244 Don Foley.

Series Designer: Tahara Anderson
Series Editor: Brian Belval